The role of higher education in providing opportunities for South Asian women

This publication can be provided in other formats, such as large print, Braille and audio. Please contact: Communications, Joseph Rowntree Foundation, The Homestead, 40 Water End, York YO30 6WP. Tel: 01904 615905. Email: info@jrf.org.uk

Available in other formats

The role of higher education in providing opportunities for South Asian women

Paul Bagguley and Yasmin Hussain

JOSEPH ROWNTREE
FOUNDATION

First published in Great Britain in 2007 by

The Policy Press
Fourth Floor, Beacon House
Queen's Road
Bristol BS8 1QU
UK

Tel no   +44 (0)117 331 4054
Fax no   +44 (0)117 331 4093
Email   tpp-info@bristol.ac.uk
www.policypress.org.uk

Published for the Joseph Rowntree Foundation by The Policy Press

ISBN 978 1 86134 973 6

British Library Cataloguing in Publication Data
A catalogue record for this book is available from the British Library.

Library of Congress Cataloging-in-Publication Data
A catalog record for this book has been requested.

Paul Bagguley is a senior lecturer in sociology and **Yasmin Hussain** is a lecturer in sociology, both in the School of Sociology and Social Policy, University of Leeds.

The **Joseph Rowntree Foundation** has supported this project as part of its programme of research and innovative development projects, which it hopes will be of value to policy makers, practitioners and service users. The facts presented and views expressed in this report are, however, those of the authors and not necessarily those of the Foundation.

Cover design by Qube Design Associates, Bristol
Printed in Great Britain by Latimer Trend, Plymouth

Contents

List of tables and figures

Tables

Figures

Acknowledgements

We would like to thank the many people who made the research reported here possible. First and foremost thanks should go to the many young South Asian women who we interviewed as well as the widening participation and careers service officers who we spoke to. We were supported over the years by three successive research managers at the Joseph Rowntree Foundation: Mark Hinman, Chris Goulden and Helen Barnard. We also benefited from the support of an advisory group throughout the research, and we would particularly like to thank Sabani Banerjee of HEFCE, Dr David Owen, Dr Andrew Pilkington, Dr Yunas Samad, Dr Peter Sanderson and Dr Laura Turney for their efforts. Aisha Siddiqah and Rahena Mossabir helped with interviewing, and the interviews were transcribed by Jodie Dyson, Marie Ross, Nichola Hutchinson, Angela Jackman, Rukshana Shah, Renata Muncey, Sanam Nazir and Louise Williams. Jodie Dyson also provided support for the organisation of advisory groups meetings. We would also like to thank Helen May and Helene Pierson of the Faculty of Education Social Sciences and Law Research Support Office at the University of Leeds for the financial management of the project.

Summary

This project was designed to examine the diversity of South Asian women's experiences of higher education (HE) and the apparent continuing barriers they face getting to university and into the labour market after graduation. It is important to recognise the diversity of South Asian women's experiences of HE in terms of their parents' origins – from Bangladesh, India and Pakistan – their social class origins and their families' educational backgrounds. This is most evident from the differences in participation in HE between the three ethnic groups where: Indian women's participation is high but growing moderately; Pakistanis women's participation is moderate but growing rapidly; and Bangladeshi women's participation is low but growing rapidly. Women in all three groups have increased their participation in HE more rapidly than White women since the early 1990s. Furthermore, 53.9% of young Indian women under the age of 30 have degrees compared with 29.7% of White women in the same age group. However, only 25.6% of young Pakistani women have degrees and only 15.5% of Bangladeshi women under 30 do so.

However, South Asian women, especially Bangladeshi and Pakistani women, remain among the most excluded and lowest-paid sections of the labour force. For example, in 2001 over 40% of Bangladeshi women without degrees were unemployed compared with only 6.7% of White women. For those with degrees the figures are much lower, with only 8.2% of Bangladeshi women graduates unemployed, but only 2.4% of White women graduates unemployed (Clark and Drinkwater, 2005).

The vast majority of Bangladeshi and Pakistani women getting to university are from manual working-class backgrounds or have fathers who are long-term sick, disabled or retired. People from such social class backgrounds have been the main target of national attempts to widen participation in higher education (Reay et al, 2005). While it appears that HE can have a strong positive role to play for enabling Bangladeshi and Pakistani women to find a route out of poverty when they graduate, they remain disadvantaged in the labour market. They are less likely to be employed in professional and managerial jobs than White women and Indian women.

The aim of this report is to explore these different patterns of participation in HE among South Asian women and to seek out explanations for some of these paradoxes. Research was carried out in Leeds and Birmingham to address the following issues:

- the barriers to entering university facing different groups of young South Asian women;
- the needs of different groups of young South Asian women prior to university, during their time at university and affecting their successful exit from university into viable careers;
- the individual and institutional strategies that are effective in enabling different groups of young South Asian women to gain access to university;
- different groups of young South Asian women's experiences of 'segregated' universities, particular types of qualification, and subject areas, and the processes giving rise to this segregation between universities.

Interviews were carried out with young Indian, Bangladeshi and Pakistani women in Sixth Forms, universities and among recent graduates. Further interviews were carried out with widening participation officers and careers service employees in universities. This qualitative data was contextualised with an analysis of official statistical sources from the

Census of Population, UCAS (Universities and Colleges Admissions Service), the Youth Cohort Study and HESA (Higher Education Statistics Agency).

The findings showed that the growth in university participation among young South Asian women across all three groups is due to their high occupational aspirations and high levels of parental support. Pioneer women in the early 1990s successfully applying to and then graduating from university from local minority ethnic communities were important role models for current students from Bangladeshi and Pakistani communities.

However, many young women from Bangladeshi and Pakistani backgrounds experienced barriers in terms of parents preferring their daughters to remain living at home while studying at university. Many young Bangladeshi and Pakistani women negotiate their way to university, balancing their desire to go to university with their parents' expectations that they will be married soon afterwards. Often reflecting parental and community expectations, many South Asian women choose subjects at degree level that reflect preferences for traditional professions, or what are seen as disciplines that are comparable in status such as Business Studies.

Certain universities are preferred because they offer the types of degree course attractive to South Asian communities, or they often ask for lower A-level scores. Students also follow the advice of successful relatives and family friends and choose the same universities as they attended. Some universities are seen as having a 'critical mass' of minority ethnic students, having a more multicultural and welcoming attitude towards South Asian students. Students in those institutions and courses without a 'critical mass' of minority ethnic students were more likely to feel isolated, and to experience racism from staff and students.

Analysis of national-level statistics showed that Bangladeshi and Pakistani female graduates are much less likely to have graduate-level jobs than White women. Careers officers, students and graduates suggested that this was partly due to limited options for geographical mobility due to family commitments. Successful access to university for South Asian women from communities with previously low levels of participation depends on:

- access to courses locally that South Asian women want to study;
- overcoming assumptions in communities, schools, universities and among employers that South Asian women from certain communities are not serious about HE;
- universities maintaining established widening participation links with local communities and related careers service work for female South Asian students and graduates;
- local communities recognising the value of a wider range of degree subjects that young women could be encouraged to apply for;
- developing role models and a critical mass of students within institutions to enable students to feel comfortable and that their university belongs to them;
- institutions ensuring that equality and diversity policies are seen to be delivered on the ground by successfully challenging unacceptable behaviour from staff and students.

Finally, this research has emphasised the fact that increasing participation in higher education is only the first step. This has to be translated into better longer-term labour market outcomes for South Asian women, especially those from Bangladeshi and Pakistani backgrounds.

Introduction

1

This report is concerned with young South Asian women's experiences of higher education (HE). We examine why more South Asian women are staying on in education and going to university than ever before and what is happening to them after graduation. These issues are of current considerable policy concern as, while many more young South Asian women are staying on in HE, there are concerns about their concentration in certain institutions (Shiner and Modood, 2002), and mounting evidence that women of Bangladeshi and Pakistani origin in particular remain disadvantaged in the labour market relative to White women even when they have a degree (EOC, 2006; Lindley et al, 2006; Peach, 2006; Platt, 2006). Bangladeshi and Pakistani women are often seen as one of the most excluded and disadvantaged groups in the labour market. These women have the lowest levels of labour market participation, and the lowest levels of educational qualifications (Bhopal, 1997a), although this situation is changing rapidly (EOC, 2006).

While there have been some previous studies of South Asian women and education, none has previously attempted to compare women of Indian, Pakistani and Bangladesh origin, and consider their situations in the Sixth Form, during their degrees and after they have graduated. There are still some myths and stereotypes about young South Asian women, especially those who are Muslim, where some do not expect them to continue into HE. Our research sets out to understand the wider context of the increasing success of South Asian women in HE.

Previous research

Previous research on this group has treated them as part of a larger group of minority ethnic students (for example, Modood and Shiner, 1994; Connor et al, 2004); has focused on particular groups of South Asian women students, such as Bangladeshis and Pakistanis alone (for example, Dale et al, 2002); or has relied on very small samples as part of wider studies of South Asian women and employment (Ahmad et al, 2003). Others have focused on Muslims alone to the neglect of ethnicity (Afshar, 1994; Ahmad, 2001). Our study includes groups of young women from Bangladeshi, Indian and Pakistani backgrounds before, during and after HE in 'old' universities as well as 'new' universities. We are thus able to draw out the differences among South Asian women in terms of ethnicity, religion and social class origins.

Young South Asian women are a critically important group to consider for several reasons. First and foremost, women of Bangladeshi and Pakistani origin have the lowest wages of any group of women of any ethnic origin (Leslie and Drinkwater, 1999). Furthermore, 60% of Bangladeshis and Pakistanis are in the lowest fifth of the income distribution, worse than any other ethnic group (Platt, 2002).

Second, although women of Bangladeshi and Pakistani origin have one of the fastest rates of increase in participation in HE, they still remain among the most excluded groups from university education. It is this combination of the UK's most severe social and economic exclusion combined with rapid change in an apparently positive direction that makes this research important.

Previous studies utilising official statistical sources have found significant differences in participation between ethnic groups, in relation to both institutions and subjects. African, African-Asian, Chinese and Indian groups have all been found to have higher percentages with degrees than the White group (Jones, 1993; Modood and Shiner, 1994; Owen et al, 1997; Shiner and Modood, 2002). The analyses by Modood and Shiner (1994; see also Shiner and Modood, 2002) suggested that the ethnic differences in the rates of success cannot be fully explained by A-level grades (actual or predicted), the number of A-levels taken, the number of sittings attended, patterns of application, or sociodemographic profile. The lower rates of success of minority ethnic groups in gaining an offer from an 'old' university leave open the possibility that some of the differences may be due to discrimination. Evidence of racial discrimination has also been uncovered in the past in admissions to medical schools. South Asian students in particular were seen to be disadvantaged due to racial discrimination using their surnames as ethnic markers (McManus et al, 1995, 1998).

The children of parents with HE normally go on to university (Modood et al, 1997). Yet Anwar (1998) found that great emphasis was placed on education by South Asian parents irrespective of their level of education. High rates of unemployment for South Asians, especially those without qualifications, and the knowledge that minority ethnic groups suffer much higher rates of unemployment are further reasons for the high stay-on rates in HE (Modood et al, 1997).

Others have attempted to examine the relationship between ethnicity, gender and educational achievement (for example, Wilson, 1978; Westwood and Hoffman, 1979; Tanna, 1990; Penn and Scattergood, 1992; Wade and Souter, 1992; Ghuman, 1994). However, the bulk of these have focused on school attainment. The existence and nature of ethnic and gender differences in attainment in national qualifications are significant factors in determining future prospects, and are of particular relevance to equality of access to such opportunities. The barrier preventing wider participation in HE, according to Seth (1985), is that South Asian women receive little support from careers officers with these cautious attitudes reflecting unfounded stereotyped images of their home background.

Others have emphasised the role of the community and the family as constraints on South Asian women's education and employment. South Asian women are presented in the popular imagination, and some academic texts, as meek, mild and docile, burdened by family pressures with no hope of pursing their ambitions and desires (Kalra, 1980; Afshar, 1994; Khanum, 1995). Obstacles hindering progression are highlighted in this literature not as external factors such as the education system but within the home and their community. Having greater domestic responsibilities and less freedom to pursue leisure activities are further deemed indicative of these women's experiences. Shaw's (1994) research on the Pakistani community in Oxford demonstrated that while only a small minority of girls gained higher qualifications, they stayed within the community, finding few problems in combining a career with an arranged marriage and participation in family and community events. However, Bhopal's (1997b, 2000) research found an inverse relationship between educational levels and the acceptance of arranged marriages and the practice of dowries. Dale et al's (2002) study also found higher levels of labour market participation for Pakistani and Bangladeshi women who had higher qualifications. Shaw's (1994) findings that only a few Pakistani young women went on to university and Kalra's (1980) account of young Sikh women leaving school at 16, contrasts with the findings of recent research that demonstrates increasing levels of participation in both HE and employment (Ahmad, 2001; Dale et al, 2002; Abbas, 2004).

Choices over the uptake of post-compulsory education for South Asian young women are much more complex than for their male counterparts or their White counterparts. South Asian women's educational and employment choices are influenced not just by qualifications, but also by cultural expectations and family and community pressures. Therefore an understanding of the perceptions of community values and the general context in which these young women take decisions about marriage, family formation and employment is relevant and important (Ahmad, 2001; Dale et al, 2002).

Factors such as religion, country of birth and the presence of children in the household are particularly relevant for South Asian women's decisions about education and employment. The family is an important institution within the South Asian community and influential on decisions made by its members (Dale et al, 2002, 2006). According to Ahmad et al (2003), the family is an important source of support for young women pusuing HE or a career. The vast majority of parents want their children to do well and encourage them for a higher standard of education (Anwar, 1998; Bhatti, 1999).

Some studies have suggested that there is a gender differentiation in parental support, with mothers keener to see their daughters succeed academically and professionally than fathers. Many older women without formal qualifications themselves are keen for their daughters to succeed academically and professionally (Bhatti, 1999). In contrast to these findings, more recent research has identified the positive role played by fathers – a finding which challenges stereotypes of 'restrictive' Asian fathers (Ahmad, 2003). For some women and their families, a positive consequence of HE and economic activity are improved marriage prospects and greater choices in issues of marriage (Ahmad et al, 2003).

For much of the Bangladeshi and Pakistani community in Britain it is important that girls should avoid any behaviour that might damage the family honour (*izzat*) (Kalra, 1980; Brah, 1993; Afshar, 1994; Joly, 1995; Bhopal, 1997a, 1997b, 2000). The continuation of post-16 education for girls places them in situations where parents are not able to police the activities of their daughters. Young women often engage in a process of negotiation with parents that, at least for some, results in being allowed to continue in education. Continuing in further education between 16 and 18 within their area of residence poses less of a threat than going outside. Traditional Asian dress signifies that a girl subscribes to the values and codes of behaviour of their community, providing an assurance to parents that could be used in negotiating permission to attend college (Dale et al, 2002).

Previous research has thus demonstrated the significance of both ethnic difference and gender in relation to HE and employment for South Asian women. Furthermore, it has identified a series of potential factors within the institutions of HE and within minority ethnic communities that contribute to the various patterns and outcomes that the research has identified.

Methodology of the present study

We aimed to find out about:

- the barriers to HE facing different groups of young South Asian women;
- the individual and institutional strategies that are effective in enabling different groups of young South Asian women gain access to HE;
- the needs of different groups of young South Asian women prior to HE, during their time in HE and enabling their successful exit from HE into viable careers;
- different groups of young South Asian women's experiences of 'segregated' HE institutions, particular types of qualification, and subject areas;
- the processes giving rise to this segregation in HE;

- how far achieving a HE qualification enables young South Asian women to be socially and geographically mobile and to gain employment;
- the strategies of key gatekeepers in advising young South Asian women about their HE options;
- their diverse experiences in the appropriate cultural, gender and familial contexts.

We interviewed young women of Bangladeshi, Indian and Pakistani and background in the Sixth Form, during their time at university and when recently graduated. We asked about their views and experiences of education; the impact of this on their family lives; their identity, including interaction with parents, siblings and the wider family; peer networks; and the role of characteristics such as gender, age and ethnicity to their experience and aspirations and plans for the future. In addition we reviewed what had been written before on these issues by other researchers, looked at the relevant official statistics, and interviewed careers and widening participation professionals for their views about young South Asian women's education as well as policy and practice in this area.

Two research sites – Birmingham and Leeds – were chosen after an examination of data from the 2001 Census of Population and a consideration of the types of university located in the cities. Both Leeds and Birmingham have 'Russell Group' universities as well as large 'new' universities. Leeds was the principal research location where a majority of the interviews took place. The research in Birmingham involved interviewing fewer people but with the same questions in order to validate the findings from Leeds. We found no noticeable differences in the qualitative interviews between the two cities, and we have reported the results in terms of the main issues and factors rather than separately for the two cities.

Table 1.1 provides details of the overall sizes of the main South Asian ethnic groups compared with the White group in Leeds and Birmingham from the Census of Population for 1991 and 2001.

We interviewed 114 young women in all, of whom 26 were Bangladeshi, 37 were Indian and 51 were Pakistani (see Table A1 in the Appendix for further details). Around a third of them were still in the Sixth Form (39), a third at university (43) and a third were recent graduates (32). The interviews were anonymised, and those interviewed were asked to choose their own pseudonyms, which have been used when quoting from interviews. Interviewees were approached in a variety of ways. Undergraduates and current sixth-formers were largely approached in the public social areas of their institutions. Some current postgraduates were also contacted in this way. In addition, Bangladeshi students and recent graduates were contacted through local community centres. The samples were

Table 1.1: Selected ethnic groups in Leeds and Birmingham, 1991 and 2001 (%)

| | Leeds | | Birmingham | |
	1991	2001	1991	2001
White	94.2	91.9	78.5	70.4
Indian	1.5	1.7	5.3	5.7
Pakistani	1.4	2.1	6.9	10.7
Bangladeshi	0.3	0.4	1.3	2.1
Other ethnic groups	2.8	5.2	8	11.2
All people (number)	680,722	715,402	961,041	977,087

Source: Census of Population 1991 and 2001, ONS

further boosted through 'snowball sampling'. The women were interviewed in places of their own choosing.

We looked at a wide range of statistical sources that could tell us what has been happening nationally in relation to South Asian women's education and their employment. These sources were the 1991 and 2001 Census of Population, HESA (Higher Education Statistics Agency) statistics, UCAS (Universities and Colleges Admissions Service) statistics and the Youth Cohort Study.

Finally, we interviewed a range of careers and widening participation officers. These ranged from those who had worked with South Asian students for some time, to those who had very limited knowledge and understanding of this group.

The structure of the report

The next chapter of this report provides a brief overview of the position of young South Asian women in employment based on our analysis of official statistical sources and the findings of other studies. Chapter 3 examines how the young women decided to go to university. This looks at issues such as which type of university they preferred, their choice of degree subject and whether or not they decided to remain at home or not while at university. We also explore the influences on these decisions, such as the views of parents, siblings and the community. Chapter 4 explores in more detail the young women's experiences of university, including the highly topical issue of student finance. Chapter 5 looks at the perspectives of professionals in HE who have contact with South Asian women at the points at which they are making important decisions about their education and careers. These are widening participation officers, and those who work in university careers centres. The final chapter provides a summary of our main findings together with some specific recommendations for policy makers and for further research.

2

The context

People of Bangladeshi or Pakistani origin are among the poorest in the UK, as shown in Figure 2.1. This shows the proportion of individuals in the bottom two fifths of the income distribution by ethnic group. There is a declining percentage of people of Indian origin in the bottom two fifths of the income distribution. In comparison, there are stable percentages of individuals from a Pakistani or Bangladeshi background in the bottom two fifths during this period. The proportion of White individuals in this position is also stable.

Women of Pakistani or Bangladeshi origin are among the lowest paid in the workforce, indeed the data suggest that their median hourly pay actually fell between 1998 and 2004 (see Table 2.1). The analysis of the Low Pay Commission (2005, p 118) concluded that there was no ethnic pay gap among full-time female employees. This suggests that the overall differences in median earnings between ethnic groups are due to part-time employment. Thus, the Low Pay Commission concluded that women in the Pakistani/Bangladeshi category are among the lowest paid because they are more likely to be employed part time.

Taken as a whole, South Asian women are much less likely to be economically active than White women (see Figure 2.2). Among those aged 16 to 24, White women are more likely to be in employment or looking for work. Indian women are more likely to

Figure 2.1: Percentage of all individuals in bottom two fifths of income distribution (before housing costs) by selected ethnic groups, Britain, 1994–2005

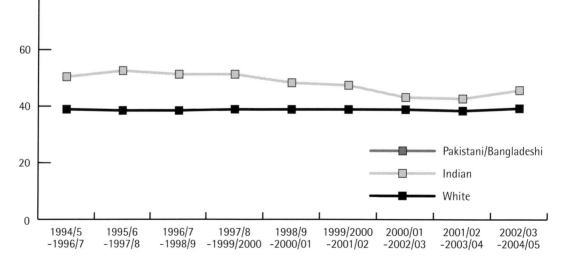

Source: DWP (2006)

Table 2.1: Median hourly pay for employees aged 18 and over by ethnicity and sex, 1998 and 2004 (£ per hour)

	1998		2004	
	Men	Women	Men	Women
White	7.19	5.39	9.31	7.06
Black	6.00	5.66	7.00	8.27
Indian	7.92	5.05	9.56	7.60
Pakistani/Bangladeshi	4.93	6.62	6.25	6.24

Source: Low Pay Commission (2005: tables 4.6 and 4.7)

Figure 2.2: Economic activity rates for selected ethnic groups by age and gender

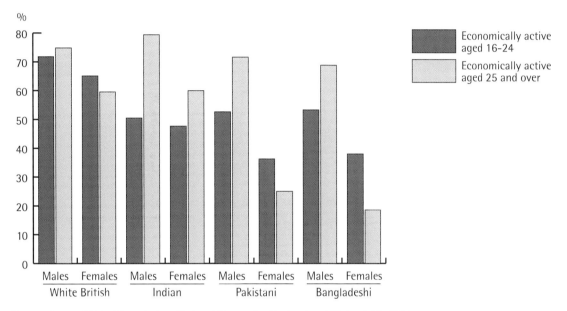

Source: Census 2001 of Population, National Report for England and Wales, table S108

be economically active at this age than Pakistani or Bangladeshi women. Among those aged 25 or over, however, Indian and White women have almost identical economic activity rates. However, only a quarter of Pakistani women in this age group are working or looking for work, and only 18% of Bangladeshi women are doing so. These findings confirm those of other researchers (Dale et al, 2002, 2006; EOC, 2006).

Pakistani women and Bangladeshi women aged 16 to 24 are much more likely to be unemployed. In contrast, White women and Indian women are more likely to be in full-time employment. Furthermore, a third of the economically inactive Pakistani and Bangladeshi women in this age group are looking after the home, while economically inactive White women and Indian women are much more likely to be students. Among those aged 25 and over Pakistani and Bangladeshi women are also more likely to be unemployed if they are economically active, and are more likely to be looking after the home if they are economically inactive (see Table A2 in the Appendix). There is considerable debate about the reasons for this, but it is likely that for older women a combination of lack of suitable qualifications, language skills for first generation migrants, marriage and childcare responsibilities and lack of opportunities in their local labour markets all play a role (Brah, 1993).

To what extent does HE affect economic activity and unemployment? Those with HE qualifications have lower levels of unemployment (see Table 2.2). However, unemployment rates for Indian women graduates are twice those for White women, and unemployment rates for Pakistani and Bangladeshi women graduates are about four times higher. There are two important points here. First, although being a graduate massively reduces the risk of unemployment for all women in these ethnic groups, Pakistani and Bangladeshi women still experience a significant 'ethnic penalty'. Second, a more detailed analysis by Lindley et al (2006) suggests that discrimination in the labour market is the only factor that is likely to explain this.

Pakistani and especially Bangladeshi women are underrepresented in management jobs compared with White and Indian women, but tend to be overrepresented in sales occupations. Otherwise the major differences shown in Table 2.2 are between men and women in each ethnic group (see Table A3 in the Appendix).

However, those women with first degrees or their equivalent are concentrated in the highest-level jobs in terms of social class. Over 75% of highly educated White British women are in professional or managerial occupations, but only 65% of similarly qualified Indian women, and 60% of Pakistani and Bangladeshi women are in these types of position. Highly educated South Asian women are much more likely than White British women to be in skilled non-manual jobs (see Table A4 in the Appendix). This demonstrates the considerable labour market advantages that may accrue to those with a university education, however, South Asian women are less likely than their White counterparts to obtain these when they have a degree. This finding is more widely confirmed in recent research by the Equal Opportunities Commission, where employer discrimination against Bangladeshi and Pakistani women has been suggested as a major factor (EOC, 2006).

Our findings here and other recent work shows the importance of sources of diversity among South Asian women in terms of ethnic origin, class and age group. Women of Bangladeshi and Pakistani origin are still among the lowest-paid groups in the workforce. The position of Indian women is very similar to that of White British women with respect to unemployment and job level. Bangladeshi and Pakistani women are more likely to be unemployed or economically inactive compared with Indian and White women. Although younger Bangladeshi and Pakistani women are improving their labour market position, they remain significantly disadvantaged compared with the majority White population. An especially important finding is that even educated women from Bangladeshi and Pakistani backgrounds are much less likely to obtain managerial and professional jobs than Indian and White women. These findings find support from other recently published research in this field (Dale et al, 2006; EOC, 2006; Lindley et al, 2006).

Table 2.2: Unemployment rates by selected ethnic groups and highest qualification: England and Wales 2001 (%)

	Male		Female	
	No qualifications	Level 4/5	No qualifications	Level 4/5
White	9.8	3.1	6.7	2.4
Indian	11.5	4.0	9.0	5.7
Pakistani	19.3	9.6	25.3	10.9
Bangladeshi	23.1	11.6	40.6	8.2

Source: Clark and Drinkwater (2005: tables 3 and 4)

3

Deciding to go to university

In this chapter we look at how the young women decided to go to university, and the influences on their decisions. There have been relatively few studies that have considered how students choose their university. These have emphasised the importance of class factors, while ethnicity and gender are seen as secondary. For example, they suggest that middle-class students assume that they will go to university, while those from working-class backgrounds and minority ethnic communities are ambivalent and uncertain about going to university. Furthermore, it has been suggested that only middle-class parents play a role in choice of university (Reay et al, 2005, p 33).

First we examine the decision making about whether or not to go to university. This is an important step, particularly for those young women from communities where women have not entered HE in the past. Then we go on to consider the influences on deciding to remain at home or to move away while at university. Finally we look at the influences on their choice of qualification and subject. In this sense we are analysing the qualitative data in order to seek out possible explanations for some of the more striking statistical trends that we have uncovered. Where relevant we note differences between graduates, current undergraduates and those in the Sixth Form when we interviewed them, as well as differences between ethnic groups and between Muslim and non-Muslim students. However, before considering these issues we would like to briefly summarise the class and educational background of the women's parents by way of providing an overview of the sample of young women that we interviewed.

HE and social class background of interviewees

It is widely known from previous research that class background and the educational qualifications of parents influence the educational outcomes of their children (Reay et al, 2005). Furthermore, we know that the different South Asian ethnic groups have different social class profiles and experiences of education (Modood et al, 1997).

None of the women in our Bangladeshi sample of interviewees had fathers who had graduated from a British university. Less than 10% of the Pakistani women who we interviewed had fathers who had attended a British university. In contrast, around 30% of the Indian women's fathers had graduated from a university in Britain. Overall, a clear majority of both Bangladeshi and Pakistani fathers had not been to university either in the Britain or elsewhere, while almost half of the Indian fathers had done so. Only one of our Bangladeshi interviewees' mothers had been to a British university, and only slightly more of the Pakistani mothers than the Indian mothers had done so. For all three ethnic groups, 80% or more of the mothers had no experience of university.

In considering the social class background of our interviewees, the small size of our samples means that we have not been able to use any of the more elaborate classifications of social class position. Furthermore, in order to adequately represent the current economic circumstances of the women's families we have considered the categories of unemployed, retired and deceased, as well as housewife for the mothers. The middle class are largely those in professional and managerial occupations, the self-employed are almost entirely small family businesses that do not employ significant numbers and the working class are largely those in semi-skilled and unskilled manual jobs.

The Bangladeshi women overwhelmingly had fathers who were in working-class jobs, were retired or deceased. The fathers of the Indian women were mostly in employment of some kind: almost a third were in middle-class jobs, almost a fifth self-employed and over a third in working-class jobs. The Pakistani fathers had a profile that falls somewhere between the Bangladeshi and Indian fathers. Over a third were in working-class jobs of some kind, with a fifth in middle-class employment or self-employed. All of the Bangladeshi women told us that their mothers were not in employment and were 'housewives'. Over 60% of the Pakistani mothers were 'housewives', but almost a fifth of them were in some kind of middle-class employment. In contrast to this, over 40% of the Indian mothers were working in some type of working-class job, while less than a fifth were reported to be 'housewives'. Here we found very distinct ethnically specific profiles of economic activity.

The growth in demand for HE among young South Asian women

There has been a rapid increase in the numbers of young South Asian women going to university since 1994 (see Table 3.1). While the percentage increase in the numbers of White women going to university was 43.3% between 1994-05 and 2004-05, the percentage increase in the number of Indian women starting full-time degrees increased by 84.8%. The number of Pakistani women starting full-time undergraduate degrees had grown by 158.7% and most dramatically for Bangladeshi women by 273.7%, reflecting the small starting number of Bangladeshi women. This increase in the numbers in HE has been faster than the growth in the 18 to 24 age group for each ethnic group (see Table A5 in the Appendix).

Comparing the 25- to 29-year-olds with the older age groups shows that the proportion of those obtaining degree-level qualifications has increased with each successive age group and by a greater degree for South Asian women than for White British women (see Table 3.2). This is especially so for women of Indian origin. However, the gender gap between men and women still remains substantial among the 25-29 age group for Pakistanis and Bangladeshis.

The recent growth in the numbers of South Asian women going to university means that many of them experience being 'pioneers'. Among those we interviewed who had graduated there were several women who had been 'pioneers' – the first women within their families or even their local communities to go on to HE. The Bangladeshi women graduates in particular often talked about such pioneers within their community, and

Table 3.1: Percentage change in numbers of first year UK domiciled full-time first degree female students by ethnicity, 1994-95 to 2004-05

	White	Indian	Pakistani	Bangladeshi
Percentage increase	43.3	84.8	158.7	273.7
Number in 1994-5	98,125	3,817	1,527	388
Number in 2004-05	140,645	7,055	3,950	1,450

Source: Calculated from HESA, 2006 (table 10b)

Table 3.2: Percentage with degree level qualifications (level 4/5) by age, sex and selected ethnic groups, England and Wales, 2001

| | | Age groups | | | | |
		25–29	30–44	45–59	60–64	65 and over
British	Males	29.8	22.4	19.1	14.1	12.6
	Females	29.7	21.5	17.8	12.7	11.3
Indian	Males	56.8	39.1	28.2	32.0	31.9
	Females	53.9	31.4	21.4	16.9	11.6
Pakistani	Males	33.2	27.2	22.8	19.4	12.5
	Females	25.6	17.4	13.1	9.6	6.7
Bangladeshi	Males	24.0	19.3	17.8	19.9	9.5
	Females	15.5	10.7	12.2	7.7	4.7

Source: Census of Population, 2001, Sample of Anonymised Records[1]

remembered a time several years previously when all of the young women in their community got married at the age of 16:

'My older sister who is 29 is from a different generation from me, she is seven years older than me but there is such a big difference between my sister and me. I remember when I was a kid, no girls went further than high school, and they had to go to high school because they would have the local services onto them asking them why you're truanting. They were expected to do well in education, you know to do well in your GCSEs, but at the end of your education system it meant that you were ready for marriage. I remember a lot of girls in my sister's time who got married at 16; they went to Bangladesh straight away in that summer and got married. I remember a lot of girls working in factories, sewing and that kind of thing. My sister and her friend Aisha were the only two Bengali girls in our community that went to college.' (Fatima Begum, Bangladeshi undergraduate, Leeds)

The women who were pioneers had diverse experiences. There were those who had faced problems due to a lack of understanding of their situation from their parents and local community, and those who had problems in terms of pressure to make certain choices. With regard to the former category, they had problems first in persuading parents to allow them to go to university, and once they were studying they experienced problems in communicating to their parents the demands that university study made on them. Parents often lacked information about the university system, and frequently assumed that it was an extension of the schooling system. This created problems in particular for those involved in studying outside of the 9am to 4pm period typical of schools and colleges. The women talked about the need to 'educate' their parents about universities, and also 'parenting' their parents when it came to managing the demands of attending university. This was confirmed by one South Asian widening participation worker who told us:

'... well before in the 70s and 80s the girls would not be encouraged to go to university and they would end up working in a factory, or working from home sewing clothes and things like that, but now the parents are starting to encourage

---

[1] The Sample of Anonymised Records is a detailed 3% sample of individuals from the 2001 Census of Population. It enables users to construct their own customised tables that are not normally provided by the main Census publications.

them to go to university.... Also marriage comes into it as well as marriage is a very big factor.... Now girls have open dialogues with their parents whereas before they probably didn't. In the 70s and 80s they didn't have open dialogue with their parents to say well this is the advantages of studying, I would like to do this, I can get married later on. A lot of people are now getting married in their mid twenties now, it's not so much pressure to get married at 18 and so parents are coming around to the idea and are accepting it and are now letting them study more.' (IH)[2]

Having achieved their goal of studying for a degree, these pioneers seemed to be viewed in two different ways within their communities. They were seen as role models for other younger women who wished to aspire to their position, thus the pioneers set the trend of going to university for younger South Asian women. The other role they performed was as 'deviants'; those within the wider community who had not educated their daughters perceived their education as deviating from the norm. Amina Chowdhury, a Bangladeshi graduate, experienced a lot of hostility from her community:

'I had certain arrogance about my community because they did not believe in education. They did not believe women should study, even my aunty said what is the point of women studying, there is no point because they are going to get married anyway and they are going to be a housewife.' (Amina Chowdhury, Bangladeshi graduate, Leeds)

Origins and destinations: current patterns of applications and acceptances among South Asian women

Previous research has shown that some minority ethnic groups are overrepresented among applicants to university, students and graduates, while others are underrepresented (Shiner and Modood, 2002; Connor et al, 2004). However, those analyses generally did not examine the gender differences within each ethnic group. In some ethnic groups, Bangladeshis for example, young women are less likely to go to university than young men. It is this gendered dimension that we are seeking to examine here.

Young Indian and Pakistani women are more likely to apply to and get to university than young White women, while young Bangladeshi women are less likely to do so. Young White women are more likely than young White men to go to university, while the application and acceptance rates among young Indian men and women are very similar. However, there are significantly higher rates of application and acceptance to university degrees among young Bangladeshi and Pakistani men than among women from those groups (see Appendix, Tables A6 and A7).

In summary, these data appear to show that in terms of going to university young Bangladeshi women still experience an ethnic penalty, while both young Bangladeshi and Pakistani women experience a gender penalty compared with men.

There are a number of differences that can be observed between White, Indian, Pakistani and Bangladeshi female applicants. These include differences in subject choice, 'class' background, school type and acceptance rates.

---

[2] Letters in brackets at the end of some quotations have been coded, to preserve the anonymity of the interviewees.

Subject choice

There are five subject areas where South Asian female applicants disproportionately apply and gain acceptance more than White female applicants: Medicine and Dentistry, subjects allied to Medicine, Mathematical and Computer Sciences, Law, and Business and Administrative Studies (see Tables A8 and A9 in the Appendix). Together these subjects account for around a half of the South Asian women's applications and acceptances, compared with about a quarter of the White women's applications and acceptances. Young South Asian women are thus twice as likely as young White women to be aiming for admission to degrees in these subjects. Furthermore, there is very little variation between the different South Asian ethnic groups in this regard, although young Indian and Pakistani women are more likely to be interested in subjects allied to Medicine than young Bangladeshi women. These findings may reflect South Asian parents' preferences for their daughters to aim for traditional professional subjects (Abbas, 2004). This is discussed further below.

'Class' background

Young White women who get to university are more likely to be from the 'middle classes' than those from any of the South Asian groups (see Table 3.3). What is striking about the results for the South Asian groups are the high percentages from routine occupational backgrounds and those for whom the occupational background is 'unknown'. A high percentage of young Bangladeshi women also come from semi-routine occupations. The very high percentages for the unknown category may be due to the fact that this information is not provided on the UCAS form, or it may be that the parents of the young women are economically inactive due to unemployment, ill-health or retirement.

Table 3.3: Female degree acceptances, by selected ethnic groups and socioeconomic group of parents, 2005 (%)

Socioeconomic group	Ethnic origin			
	Bangladeshi	Indian	Pakistani	White
1. Higher managerial and professional occupations	3.2	12.2	6.5	17.9
2. Lower managerial and professional occupations	9.9	17.2	12.6	26.7
3. Intermediate occupations	3.4	10.5	5.7	13.1
4. Small employers and own account workers	9.2	7.3	12.7	5.9
5. Lower supervisory and technical occupations	0.3	3.4	2.3	4.1
6. Semi-routine occupations	20.2	14.4	11.0	10.8
7. Routine occupations	7.2	7.8	7.7	4.4
8. Unknown	46.7	27.3	41.5	17.1
Grand total	100.0	100.0	100.0	100.0
Total N	*1,419*	*7,019*	*4,135*	*150,537*

Note: Percentages may not total 100 due to rounding.
Source: UCAS, authors' analysis

School type

Bangladeshi and Pakistani women starting university in 2005 were more likely to have attended Sixth Form College than those of Indian or White background (see Table 3.4). A further feature that stands out is that women of Indian or White background were more likely to have attended an Independent School than those of Bangladeshi or Pakistani origin. This is important as previous research (Reay et al, 2005) has shown that Independent Schools have better support for their pupils in general when applying to university.

Table 3.4: Female degree acceptances by school and selected ethnic groups, 2005 entry (%)

| | Ethnic origin | | | |
	Bangladeshi	Indian	Pakistani	White
Comprehensive school	30.3	25.7	24.9	28.1
Further/higher education	24.2	18.4	24.5	22.0
Grammar school	2.0	4.3	2.4	6.3
Independent school	2.2	10.7	4.0	8.5
Other	1.1	1.2	2.3	1.3
Other maintained	3.1	11.1	6.5	5.1
Sixth form centre	5.4	1.3	1.3	0.6
Sixth form college	20.3	14.8	17.9	10.9
Unknown	11.3	12.5	16.1	17.3
Grand total	100.0	100.0	100.0	100.0
Total N	1,419	7,019	4,135	150,537

Note: Percentages may not total 100 due to rounding.
Source: UCAS, authors' analysis

Acceptance rates

In Table 3.5 we can see that 34.6% of White women accepted to university in 2005 had 360 or more points, 26.5% of Indian women and 18% of Pakistani women had these points, but only 14.8% of Bangladeshi women had them.[3] When compared with the findings of Shiner and Modood (2002), where they found that the higher levels of university acceptances among White applicants compared with Bangladeshis and Pakistanis was largely explained by differences in A-level scores, we can see that they operate as a significant source of inequality between ethnic groups.

---

[3] UCAS uses 'tariff bands' to summarise the educational qualifications of university entrants, and these express as a numerical scale the applicants' grades at A-level and AS-level as follows: at A-level, grade A = 120, B = 100, C = 80, D = 60 and E = 40. Equivalent grades at AS-level are half the value of these. Consequently, what are often taken as the grades required for those courses for which there is high competition are three grade As at A-level, which translate into 360 points. However, as students may have pursued more than one A-level or additional AS-levels the tariff bands are only an approximate measure of attainment. Nevertheless, if we assume that 360 points or more is equivalent to three grade As, and therefore the qualifications required for entry to the Universities of Oxford and Cambridge, or to study popular subjects such as Law in a 'Russell Group' university, it may be taken as an appropriate measure of the attainment required for the most elite universities and subjects.

Table 3.5: Tariff bands and female degree acceptances by selected ethnic groups, 2005 entry (%)

Tariff band	Ethnic origin			
	Bangladeshi (%)	Indian(%)	Pakistani (%)	White (%)
0	12.2	9.7	15.9	15.4
001–079	3.5	2.2	3.9	2.7
080–119	5.3	3.7	4.3	1.9
120–179	14.2	10.9	13.2	5.1
180–239	19.4	15.6	16.6	9.7
240–299	17.0	16.4	16.1	14.5
300–359	13.7	14.9	12.1	16.3
360–419	7.7	12.5	9.0	15.0
420–479	3.7	7.6	5.1	10.0
480–539	2.5	3.9	2.5	5.7
540 plus	0.9	2.5	1.4	3.9
Grand total	100.0	100.0	100.0	100.0
Total N	1,419	7,019	4,135	150,537

Note: Percentages may not total 100 due to rounding.
Source: UCAS, authors' analysis

For White female applicants there is a fairly clear gradient in acceptance rates from the 'middle-class' socioeconomic groups to the lower ones (see Table 3.6). However, the acceptance rates for Pakistani women are higher for those from routine occupational backgrounds than for those from 'middle-class' higher managerial and professional backgrounds. Generally speaking, for each socioeconomic group the acceptance rates for Indian women and White women are higher than those for Pakistani women. This is especially noticeable for those from 'middle-class' higher managerial and professional

Table 3.6: Acceptance rates for female applicants by selected ethnic groups and socioeconomic group of parents, 2005 entry

Socioeconomic group	Ethnic origin			
	Bangladeshi	Indian	Pakistani	White
1. Higher managerial and professional occupations	0.79[a]	0.84	0.73	0.85
2. Lower managerial and professional occupations	0.75	0.83	0.76	0.81
3. Intermediate occupations	0.77	0.81	0.72	0.78
4. Small employers and own account workers	0.82	0.83	0.76	0.78
5. Lower supervisory and technical occupations	0.50[a]	0.87	0.83[a]	0.79
6. Semi-routine occupations	0.75	0.82	0.72	0.73
7. Routine occupations	0.80	0.82	0.77	0.74
8. Unknown	0.74	0.78	0.69	0.75
All	0.76	0.81	0.72	0.79

Note: [a] Numbers of either applicants or acceptances less than 100 in these categories.
Source: UCAS, authors' analysis

backgrounds, suggesting that they have a 'class advantage' that minority ethnic students do not have. Middle-class Bangladeshi and Pakistani women experience an 'ethnic penalty' when applying to university. They are less likely to be successful in securing a place than their middle-class Indian and White peers. Shiner and Modood (2002) found that, when all other factors were taken into account, this was often due to older universities being less likely to offer places to minority ethnic applicants. However, our evidence does not enable us to demonstrate that discrimination is taking place.

Developments at GCSE and A-level

Normally two or more A-levels and five or more good GCSEs (grade C or better) are needed for university entrance.[4] Regardless of ethnic origin, women are improving at GCSE level more than men and South Asian women more than White women (see Table 3.7). In relation to these ethnic groups, Indian women were performing best at GCSE level by 1999, closely followed by Indian men. Furthermore, Indian women were the group who had improved the most between 1986 and 1999, followed by Bangladeshi women. In 1999 Bangladeshi women did almost as well as White men, but less than half of Pakistani women got five or more good GCSEs, and their improvement since 1986 was well behind that of other South Asian women. Only 37% of Pakistani women and 27.1% of Bangladeshi men obtained five or more good GCSEs in 1999.

Table 3.7: Five or more GCSEs at A*-C at end of year 11 by gender for selected ethnic groups, 1986 and 1999 (%)

	White		Indian		Pakistani		Bangladeshi	
	1986	1999	1986	1999	1986	1999	1986	1999
Males								
Five or more GCSEs A*-C	35.8	61.0	33.3	69.8	23.4	37.7	25.0	27.1
Less than five GCSEs A*-C	64.2	39.0	66.7	30.2	76.6	62.3	75.0	72.9
N	*6,091*	*5,441*	*96*	*159*	*64*	*122*	*12*	*48*
Females								
Five or more GCSEs A*-C	36.8	68.6	29.6	78.6	21.7	46.7	23.1	60.3
Less than five GCSEs A*-C	63.2	31.4	70.4	21.4	78.3	53.3	76.9	39.7
N	*6,712*	*6,490*	*115*	*215*	*46*	*169*	*13*	*58*

Source: Youth Cohort Study (1988 and 2002), authors' analysis

There is also a similar pattern of results at A-level with Indian women and men performing the best. Only one third of the Pakistani and Bangladeshi women have two or more A-levels, while only one quarter of Pakistani and Bangladeshi men have these qualifications (see Appendix, Table A10). In terms of having the basic qualifications for university entry, Bangladeshi and Pakistani women would appear to be still at a significant disadvantage compared with women from White and Indian backgrounds.

---

[4] We have carried out an analysis of the most recent Youth Cohort Study to examine this issue for young South Asian women nationally. For particular sexes in the minority ethnic groups the numbers in this survey become rather small, especially Bangladeshi women, but some important indications about developments over time and overall national patterns can be identified in the following tables.

To study for a degree or not: reasons for going to university

In this section we examine the main reasons for deciding to go to university. Large-scale surveys of minority ethnic groups in HE have found that South Asians tend to emphasise employment prospects and family encouragement as key reasons for going to university (Connor et al, 2004, p 27). This has also been found in some qualitative studies of South Asian women (Ahmad et al, 2003). Other research (Reay et al, 2005) has focused on factors influencing the choice between universities, rather than the young people's rationales for going to university in the first place. These have emphasised the class background of the students rather than ethnicity and gender. We found the following kinds of reasons given by the young women in the present study for going to university:

- 'natural progression';
- economic reasons: job, salary, status;
- independence;
- parental wishes;
- wanting to become better mothers and members of their own communities;
- a desire for education and personal development;
- following role models;
- delaying marriage.

Individual women would often give several of these reasons, however, there were clear patterns in relation to their ethnic origins and religion. Indian women often spoke of a natural progression into HE that was assumed by both their parents and their schools. However, Bangladeshi and Pakistani women tended have more complex and overlapping sets of reasons for HE. While they were encouraged to consider university by their parents, it was often not assumed to be a 'natural progression' for them by their schools. For Bangladeshi and Pakistani women, economic reasons, wanting to become better mothers and members of their own communities, a desire for education and personal development, and role models were very important. The Bangladeshi women in particular were more likely to give instrumental or economic reasons for going to university. They had their eyes on their longer-term careers, and obtaining better paid employment than their parents had been able to do. Pakistani women also often gave these longer-term career goals as the reason for wanting to go to university, but like some of the Bangladeshi women they were also motivated to fulfil their parents' wishes, to take up opportunities that had been denied their parents as economic migrants, and to study for reasons of self-fulfilment as well as contributing to their own communities.

A natural progression

All of the Indian students currently at university talked about HE as being a natural progression from the Sixth Form. Many of the young Indian women said that this was the assumption in their family from their parents.

> 'In my case everybody, all of my siblings had all gone to university and generally with outside of my family as well there was an assumption that everybody was going to go to university so I never saw it as an option, it was just something that was going to happen....' (Jeevan Mudan, Indian graduate, Leeds)

Furthermore, the schools and colleges and that they attended also seemed to assume that they would go to university. As Isha Sharma, an Indian undergraduate, told us: "It's one of those things that is always drummed into you, not just from your parents but from school too."

This assumption was also found in some of the Bangladeshi and Pakistani households, as Jasmin Ali, a Pakistani Muslim university student, said: "It wasn't even an option, it's just like you're going to go to Uni afterwards … because you have older cousins and stuff you know you're going Uni as well". However, one further reason given for the strong parental support for going on into HE among some Bangladeshi parents was that they recognised that in Britain their daughters had opportunities for HE that their parents as adult migrants from Bangladesh did not have. Jabeen Ahmad, a Bangladeshi Muslim undergraduate, explained these reasons behind her parents encouraging her: "They haven't been educated back home, they know an education for us here is important". Early parental support and expectations were crucial for the decision to apply for university.

However, the Indian women often mentioned that this expectation came from both the home and the school. The Bangladeshi and Pakistani women tended to mention parental support alone, often in terms of taking up opportunities that they themselves did not have.

Economic reasons

There were a number of dimensions to the economic reasons for going to university. For some it entailed simple social mobility; their university degree would enable them to obtain a better job. However, this was also often linked to using their education and career to benefit their families and communities. Most of these were Bangladeshi and Pakistani:

> 'Because I believe that in this day and age you have to have some kind of education otherwise we will be stuck in clerical or admin jobs and that hasn't got a lot of money or anything like that, so really it's about, at the end of the day, whatever we do, it's always about money.' (Jabeen Ahmad, Bangladeshi undergraduate, Leeds)

Independence

Another aspect expressed by many women was the desire for some kind of independence, in the sense of a transition into adulthood that comes with leaving the parental home:

> 'I wanted independence. I wanted to live away from home. I wanted the lifestyle because my sister went to university, she has this influx of money and she was in a massive city because we come from a very small town and I thought, wow, that really looks good and I really want to try it.' (Simi Banu, Indian undergraduate, Leeds)

Parents' wishes

Some of the women wanted to pursue an education so that they can fulfil their parents' wishes. These desires on the part of parents are not just for their daughters to obtain a degree, but are frequently expressed as a desire for their daughter to enter one of the established professions such as Medicine or Law:

> 'My mum likes to call me a solicitor already, she goes "Oh yeah, someone is training to be a solicitor". Of all the children, my mum is the proudest of me in that sense, my mum values all their degrees but because I'm doing Law it's a bit different.' (Fatima Begum, Bangladeshi undergraduate, Leeds)

Becoming better members of the community

Others talked about the importance of education to their future role as parents and adult members of their own communities. This is an aspect of choosing to go to university that has perhaps been overlooked previously, and one that might be especially important for minority ethnic communities:

> 'If you've got a good education and you've got good knowledge you can educate your children then and the community and also you are seen as a role model so there are other people who will benefit from your knowledge and experience.' (Jabeen Ahmad, Bangladeshi undergraduate, Leeds)

Education and personal development

There were some women who had a strong desire to learn, to study as an end in itself. According to these women it was a personal desire to study that drove them. They described in enthusiastic terms the sense of personal growth and independence that this has given them:

> 'It's a drive! Something drives you. It's like if I can pick up a book and think oh my god I'm really excited I really want to read this book, then I know I've got something inside me which is like pushing me … I did my A-levels I really enjoyed it, I loved doing all the work … so I thought ok I feel ready for the Uni life now, I'm a bit independent, I need to get a bit more and I can work on my own.' (Fareena Anjum, Pakistani graduate, Leeds)

Role models

Other people who had been to university who acted as role models were important for most of the women who we interviewed. The most frequently cited role models were older sisters, cousins or friends of the family in the community. These role models were often important sources of information about how to apply to university and potential careers, as well as bargaining with reluctant parents. However, in a few instances such role models were not local but 'transnational', reflecting the increasingly importance of HE for women in South Asia:

> 'My cousins even in Pakistan have all gone into further education they are either doing medicine or doing really good things and it is amazing really because you think we're sat here with all the opportunities that are available to us and they're sat in Pakistan, why not take these opportunities.' (Shameem Khan, Pakistani undergraduate, Leeds)

Marriage decisions and going to university

Marriage was central to the plans of young women from all of the South Asian communities. It was related to decisions about education in quite specific ways that are quite unlike the majority White population. For most of the Indian students marriage planning was not such a current concern, but for many of the Bangladeshi and Pakistani women decisions around marriage and negotiations with their parents about this were more central. A few had married before going to university. Some saw marriage as a risk that could disrupt their education at any point. However, most had deferred their marriage until they completed their degrees.

Within the South Asian communities there has been evidence that the attitudes of young South Asians on 'arranged' marriages are shifting from those of their parents (Stopes-Roe and Cochrane, 1990; Anwar, 1998). This was found to be more the case among Sikhs and Hindus than among South Asian Muslims (Modood et al, 1997). This was reflected in the interviews with Sikh and Hindu young women in this study. They did not see marriage as being either their decision or their parents'. Their choice was a mixture of both. However, among Muslim women it was clear that changes are moving in the same direction as the Hindu and Sikh communities. Although some young women talked about 'arranged marriage', modifications have been made to this practice, so that it is more appropriate to talk of 'negotiated marriage'.

For some of those studying A-levels their decisions about education were seen as dictated by their impending marriage. In some instances these women were aware their marriages were being arranged by their parents. Some of them, especially the Bangladeshi and Pakistani women, said that they might have to pull out of their education at any time. While most parents placed a major importance on education, there were others who were the complete opposite. Consequently, their daughters were unable to make firm decisions on their future with respect to education:

> 'I am hoping they find someone after my studies, 'cos then I can just concentrate on my studies, if they find someone in the middle of my education then it will probably ruin it.' (Alpha Rehman, Bangladeshi sixth-former, Leeds)

According to Amina Chaudhury, a Bangladeshi graduate in Leeds who refused to get married before completing her degree, her parents were currently looking for a husband for her. However, this was proving difficult, as she argues that having an educated daughter-in-law is perceived as a threat by some in her community: "A lot of people are daunted by the experience of women having a degree because they are a lot more articulate".

We also encountered some young women who had come out of the education system early, but then chose to re-enter it. Zoreena Bibi, a Bangladeshi graduate, was taken to Bangladesh at the age of 16 and married, but she went back into education as a part-time student: "I felt I was missing something and I realised that education is so important you can't go anywhere without education and I always dreamt of doing a degree". However, there were relatively few instances of this route into HE, as most of the young women were deferring their marriages until after they had graduated. Indeed, they chose education as a way of deferring marriage.

For the young women of Indian descent, their discussion of 'arranged' marriage involved far more negotiation with their parents, although 'love' marriages were also favoured within these groups and to some extent allowed. For the Indian young women, in general parents avoided the subject of marriage until their daughters finished their degrees and even then the young women negotiated more time with their parents to allow them to set up their careers:

> 'They know that after university I will be going home. They have mentioned to me in a few months they will start looking and I have told them no as I don't want to get married for a least a couple of years yet. I want to get settled in my career, progress to where I want to be, be satisfied with who I am and then get married I think … they don't have much choice in the matter really.' (Saman Kaur, Indian undergraduate, Leeds)

It is within the Pakistani sample where there is the most evidence of changes of opinion and practice taking place between generations. Traditional parentally or family arranged marriages seem to be in decline. Instead, consultation and negotiation now take place between the parents and their child. The Pakistani young women saw this shift as a new freedom because of the contrast to past restrictions where either siblings or friends had experienced a more strict and restrictive form of arranged marriage.

There was also a definite class difference among the Pakistani sample in relation to views about marriage. Those from a higher-class background would point out the differences between their families who were educated and in professional jobs in comparison to how families who were less educated and in manual jobs. When asked what type of marriage they would like, most of the Pakistani young women talked about a negotiated marriage. What was interesting to note here was that although marriage was something that was seen as inevitable by the young women, they were adamant on pursuing education irrespective of marriage:

> 'Even if I was going to get, you know, married in the next three years, I'm still thinking of carrying on with what I'm wanting to do not just to stop because you are married or whatever.' (Farhana Sheikh, Pakistani sixth-former, Leeds)

There were some cases when students were already married and were pursuing their education after marriage. In many instances this was the 'contract' that was made before marriage between the woman's parents and her husband's family. There were a number of reasons given for this. According to Rafika Amin, a Pakistani in a Leeds Sixth Form, who is married and now living with her in-laws' family, these concerned the moral risks of going to university: "At Uni you get led on by people ... you do stupid things ... I want to know when I go home at the end of the day I have somebody at home waiting for me".

Leaving home or living at home?

Studying at university for some South Asian women involves a critical decision not only about which university and which course, but also about whether or not to stay at home with their parents or move away to study. In the more general literature on university choice it is assumed that those from working-class backgrounds and minority ethnic groups have either limited economic resources, limited knowledge about their choices or choose the local university as it suits people like themselves (Reay et al, 2005, pp 86-96). Others have noted that some South Asian Muslim female students might encounter parental preferences for them to remain at home while attending university (Dale et al, 2002; Connor et al, 2004). We have found this to be one of the most important factors differentiating Muslim from non-Muslim women.

Many of the widening participation and careers officers who we interviewed felt that young South Asian women were strongly influenced by parents and location in their choice of university. We found that this was the case in the West Midlands as well as in Yorkshire. This also had disadvantages for those students who were pursuing 'sandwich' courses, which required a job placement. Often students are required to be geographically mobile to take up such placements, and South Asian women were one category of students seen to be disadvantaged by their relative geographical immobility:

> 'I don't think they choose universities by thinking this university is good for this subject and another would be good for that reason. They just go there because it's convenient and a lot of them just go there because their parents won't allow them to go to a university that is away from home.' (Widening participation officer, IH)

However, such bold statements obscure a more complex and differentiated picture of negotiation. Perhaps the most important distinction is between Muslim and non-Muslim students. All of the Bangladeshi and Pakistani students identified themselves as Muslims, whereas a majority of the Indian women identified themselves as Hindus or Sikhs. Almost all of the non-Muslim Indian students currently at university appeared to have had the option of leaving home. These women did talk about the reservations of their families, in particular their parents, about them leaving home. However, these reservations were a more significant issue for the Muslim women of Indian, Bangladeshi or Pakistani background.

For the Muslim respondents, leaving home to study away would involve considerable negotiation with their parents, and those who did move away from the family home to study often faced considerable obstacles in persuading their parents to agree. According to Sadia Hussain, a Pakistani Muslim, "There is stuff going on at home and you get away from all that stuff. It's like a fresh start", but she failed to convince her parents to let her move away to go to university. Similar sentiments were aired by Fatima Begum, a Bangladeshi Muslim, who encountered problems in convincing her mother to allow her to leave home to study given what the rest of the community would think. Thus, the opposition comes not only from parents, but is partly due to the parents' fear of disapproval or loss of face among the local community: "It is out of the ordinary from what the community does, she had to think about what the people would think ... with being an Asian girl you are kind of preferred to stay close to home...."

For some of the young women leaving home was not always all that important and did not involve conflict or negotiation with parents. Jabeen Ahmad, a Bangladeshi undergraduate, cannot see the logic of moving away from home for the sake of it: "If I can get an education right on my doorstep why am I going to travel all the way to wherever?" As a result she applied only to local universities.

In general, the reasons for Muslim women studying near to their home were quite different from the reasons of finance or convenience, as suggested in previous studies focusing on White working-class students (Reay et al, 2005). For these Muslim students the main reasons were the preferences of parents and the views of the wider community. These concerns about morality, parental and community views and the family's *izzat* (honour) remain a powerful force among some sections of the Pakistani communities in Leeds and Birmingham:

> 'I don't want to go to Bradford; I don't think the family will approve of me going out of the city ... I think it's because with our family there are restrictions ... 'cos some of the women got spoilt and stuff. They start having relationships with boys and other things. When I came to college, nobody approved of me coming to college, they were like "We don't want her to ruin the family reputation", and my dad was like "I have that trust in my daughter, and they need to go out 'cos they are going to step out one day" ... I think it's only in the Mirpuri community because I think with people from the Punjab, like Lahore, the parents are educated and then it is passed on, whereas the Mirpuri, they don't tend to study.' (Hajra Khan, Pakistani sixth-former, Leeds)

This also underlines the importance of not just reading off the constraints from religion. Different cultures even from within Pakistan and different class and educational experiences come into play. It is too simple to assert that Muslim women face constraints. Rather these constraints are mediated by the need and desire for education, and changing values within the communities, as well as cultural diversity among Muslims.

However, it would be wrong to suggest that this is the only reason for young Muslim women living with their parents while they studied at university. For some of the women, remaining at home was a choice, as they valued the day-to-day support that their families could offer. According to Sobia Ali, a Bangladeshi graduate: "It was okay because it was near home, so I had time to come home as well and had family support there which was really good."

Some had applied to universities outside of their locality against their parents' wishes but were refused permission to leave home. In these exceptional cases the young women felt they were compromising the quality of their education in order to fit in with their parents' preferences. Saima Mamood, a Pakistani graduate, had a place to study Legal Executive Management at Aston University and was not allowed to go, so she enrolled at Bradford University studying Business Management instead. She told us that she regrets not having been allowed to go to Aston as she believes her life would have changed if she had gone to there:

> 'I was pressurised into either stay local or not go at all so I went to Bradford. I believe I would have been more independent … I would have been more happier and more proud that I've achieved something I wanted to do … I regret my career choice. I regret the degree I did to a large extent and now if I can go back in time I would have been more adamant and done Law … my degree didn't really help me.'

A factor often mentioned in accounts of middle-class choice of university is the depth of research that middle-class students carry out into finding the right kind of degree and institution (Reay et al, 2005). For these students it is the perceived quality of the university and the suitability of the course that determines choice of location. We found something like this among many of the Indian non-Muslim women who we interviewed, and this does perhaps reflect the more middle-class and highly educated background of the Indian women's parents. They looked in more detail at the course and the institution, and this was often a more significant factor than location in their choice of institution. Nina Patel told us that she also chose the best universities for the course she wanted to do when she applied through UCAS. That was her driving factor, not locality but the course itself.

Most of those who had graduated reflected back at length on the decisions about leaving home or staying at home to study. The non-Muslim Indian women who had graduated had generally had a wider choice of institutions than the Bangladeshi or Pakistani women. Pooja Parmar, an Indian graduate, whose parents would not have minded if she had left home, told us: "I could go anywhere I wanted to or where my degree took me to. It was my choice." However, for many of the Bangladeshi and Pakistani graduates their choice of universities was often geographically restricted. It was rare for these graduate women to have made decisions about attending universities simply based on the university itself or the nature of the course. Proximity to home was of major importance.

In this discussion we have so far focused on the constraints on the choice of undergraduate degrees that emanated from the preferences of parents of some students. However, we did encounter some graduates who faced rather different familial constraints on postgraduate degrees. For example, Jeevan Mudan, an Indian graduate living in Leeds, was single when she left home to go to Brunel University to study for her first degree, as she had a choice: "I thought I'd go out for a bit, I didn't want to stay at home". However, for her postgraduate degree she was married and it was difficult for her to leave home: "I don't think my husband would be too keen on the fact that I'm not home".

Marriage added another dimension for these women in terms of constraints; it became more difficult for the women to move away when they were married, they talked about leniency and flexibility from their parents, but they sometimes lacked the same space for negotiation with their husbands. Marriage has often featured as a factor identified in other studies limiting the labour market prospects of South Asian women graduates (Dale et al,

2002; Ahmad et al, 2003), and here it also appeared to operate as an important constraint over university choice at undergraduate and postgraduate levels.

Some young women currently in the Sixth Form said that they would prefer to stay in their parental home during university due to the complications of living on their own. In these instances their rationales for staying at home are similar to those found among White working-class students where monetary constraints and the reliance upon the experience of friends are important (Reay et al, 2005). For example:

> 'Finding a home to rent out and staying there will be a hassle. Coming home every weekend will be another hassle, I don't want to go and live somewhere else, I rather stay at home where everything is done for me … I know when people move out they find it really hard just keeping up with rent and stuff … it's a personal choice me not wanting to move out … like it's said, nothing's better than home!' (Mehwish Begum, Pakistani sixth-former)

Choosing subjects and qualifications

In this section we will examine what subjects young South Asian women apply for at university and how successful they are through an analysis of UCAS statistics. We shall then go on to consider how these choices are shaped.

Overall the acceptance rates[5] are very similar for each ethnic group, although the rate for Pakistani women is the lowest (see Table 3.8). Focusing on the five most popular subjects for South Asian women, although they have a lower acceptance rate for Medicine and Dentistry than White women, for subjects allied to Medicine it is rather better for South Asian women, especially those of Indian and Pakistani origin. For Maths and Computer Sciences there is little variation, but some evidence that Bangladeshis accept this as a 'second best option'. Law is an especially competitive subject for entry and, like Medicine, the acceptance rates are lower for South Asian applicants, especially Pakistani women, as they are for Business and Administrative Studies.

When we look at the instances where there are acceptance rates greater than 1.0 – 'the second best options' – two features emerge. First, they tend to be in combined degrees, where two or more subjects are studied. Second, South Asian students are much more likely to have taken the 'second best option'. This fits with evidence from other studies suggesting that South Asian students often re-sit GCSEs and A-levels to achieve higher grades. Shiner and Modood (2002) suggested that these re-sits were a key reason why minority ethnic students were concentrated in new universities, as established institutions where there is stronger competition for entry often did not take re-sits into account.

How do these ethnically distinctive patterns of application to university emerge? How do young South Asian women decide on different subjects and what influences them? For those still in the Sixth Form, irrespective of ethnicity, parents and families played a major role when choosing subjects and qualifications. In some instances the women

---

[5] These are more difficult to interpret than one might think. The appearance of values greater than 1.0 in the table might appear to be surprising as it suggests that more people obtained places than applied for them in the first place! However, there are three straightforward explanations for this apparent anomaly. First, applications are coded by the most frequently mentioned subject on an applicant's UCAS form. Thus an applicant might fill in most of their UCAS choices for Medicine, but actually get a place in Physical Sciences. Second, many universities might reject an applicant for one subject but offer them a place in another subject where demand is lower. Third, the numbers involved in these cases are very small, so these results should be treated with caution.

Table 3.8: Acceptance rates for female applicants by selected ethnic groups and JACS (Joint Academic Coding of Subjects) subject group, 2005 entry

	Ethnic origin			
	Bangladeshi	Indian	Pakistani	White
JACS Subject Group				
Group A Medicine & Dentistry	0.31	0.47	0.31	0.55
Group B Subjects allied to Medicine	0.64	0.78	0.74	0.63
Group C Biological Sciences	0.92	0.98	0.99	0.92
Group D Veterinary Science, Agriculture & related	0.50	3.43	5.00	0.84
Group F Physical Sciences	1.25	1.34	1.71	1.07
Group G Mathematical & Computer Sciences	1.15	1.00	0.95	0.99
Group H Engineering	1.63	1.58	1.40	1.12
Group J Technologies	0.00	2.63	5.00	2.26
Group K Architecture, Building & Planning	0.92	0.90	1.22	1.01
Group L Social Studies	0.88	0.92	0.81	0.83
Group M Law	0.84	0.86	0.79	0.92
Group N Business & Administrative studies	0.73	0.82	0.71	0.87
Group P Mass Comms and Documentation	0.74	0.91	0.91	0.93
Group Q Linguistics, Classics & related	0.93	0.87	1.08	0.94
Group R European Langs, Literature & related	0.33	0.94	0.67	0.94
Group T Non-European Languages and related	0.33	1.83	0.76	1.54
Group V History & Philosophical studies	0.97	0.99	1.00	0.92
Group W Creative Arts & Design	0.63	0.71	0.65	0.72
Group X Education	0.61	0.80	0.68	0.75
Y Combined arts	3.08	1.50	1.47	1.26
Y Combined sciences	8.50	10.40	7.83	2.64
Y Combined social sciences	2.69	2.19	2.04	1.74
Y Sciences combined with social sciences or arts	2.00	2.07	2.26	1.76
Y Social sciences combined with arts	2.58	1.63	2.35	1.41
Z General, other combined & unknown	4.43	15.00	8.91	3.89
Z No preferred subject group	0.00	0.00	0.00	0.00
All	0.76	0.81	0.72	0.79

Source: UCAS, authors' analysis

were confident about asserting their own perspectives but they still ultimately abided by their family's decision. Families generally wanted their daughters to study 'traditional' professional subjects such as Law, Medicine and Dentistry; subjects such as Sociology, English and Psychology were not seen as serious academic disciplines. The underlying logic to this was the concern for their future employment prospects; parents wanted to ensure that their child would be able to utilise their education to obtain work or for it to have value within the wider society. There were women who were confident about parental support for their chosen subjects regardless of the parents' stated preferences:

'My parents could tell me "do Medicine or Law" but they know that what I love is fashion so it would be pointless doing something else … they know I wouldn't do as well if I did a different subject.' (Salima Azar, Pakistani sixth-former, Leeds)

Almost all of those in the Sixth Forms were pursuing a conventional route to HE through A-levels. A-levels are still the traditional path to HE and were known to parents and the wider community as the most acceptable form of qualification. To some extent this is in contrast to the findings of some large-scale surveys, which suggest that minority ethnic groups disproportionately choose vocational qualifications (for example, Connor et al, 2004, p 16). Parents who were influential in choosing the A-level route for their daughters viewed it as being a better path to further education and a 'good job'. In some cases, the young women themselves also viewed A-levels in this way. Consequently, few of them followed less conventional routes such as GNVQs. Fozia Khanum, a Pakistani sixth-former, was following the advice she received from her family: "They said do your A-levels 'cos you can move on getting a good job and going to further education". Women currently at university also viewed A-levels as a more straightforward route into HE:

> 'I think A-levels are more valued rather than vocational subjects and I think I just found it a straightforward way to get into Uni … if you do these different types of courses I think it might be more difficult to get in.' (Leena Mistry, Indian undergraduate, Leeds)

However, in comparison to their certainty about the desirability of studying for A-levels if they were thinking about going to university, many of the 16- to 18-year-olds had not thought about the courses they wished to follow in HE in any great detail. For example, Tahira Bibi was choosing to do a course with childcare, having decided due to her domestic duties: "I look after my cousin at home and I got all details, so I thought childcare would be good for me".

Among those at university their parents were also more likely to have encouraged their daughters to study more traditional subjects. For instance, according to Shahida Azam, an Indian Muslim currently at university studying Broadcasting at Leeds: "You always get that pressure from family you should do engineer, doctor or lawyer, but I've just kind of ignored that 'cos I've been quite independent". Even the Pakistani women showed resistance to traditional professional subjects. According to Shazia Manzoor, a Pakistani undergraduate, her parents had wanted her to study subjects that would lead to a career in one of the traditional professions instead of Childhood Studies: "My mum wanted me to become a doctor or a solicitor 'typical' but I didn't want to be that because everybody was doing that".

In choosing their own subject some of the young women currently at university had faced objections from their parents. One such was Nina Patel who was studying Law and Communications. Her parents approved of the Law aspect of her degree, but they did not like the Communications element: "Judging from my family, they have all gone into Accountancy, Pharmacy, Dentistry". Nina had to endure her family's objections but was enjoying the course. Similarly, parents objected when their daughters changed their minds about their degrees and their subjects from the more acceptable sciences or professional qualifications to humanities and social sciences.

While some of the women went ahead with their own choices, there were others who were persuaded to do what their families had wanted, but now regretted it. The risk in cases such as this is that the students study subjects for which they may have neither the aptitude nor the enthusiasm and may therefore finish up with lower grades at A-level or a lower class of degree. Jasmine Ali's mother objected to her initial choice to do English, so she ended up studying Law. However, she now regrets that decision because she finds Law a difficult subject. She recalls her mother's reasoning as follows:

> 'She was like "It's going to be a better degree because it's more recognised because it's Law", and she was like "With English language, where are you going to get

with it?" Law is one of the hardest degrees, it's on the top, but I wish I'd done an easier degree.' (Jasmine Ali, Pakistani undergraduate, Leeds)

The encouragement to do well in education was emphasised by most of the young women who we interviewed. Such was the need for the parents to make sure that their child did well, some parents actually chose their daughters' subjects at A-level and had an important input into them choosing their degrees.

Kalpana Bharati talked about her father choosing A-levels for her that were impossible for her to pass. She did the subjects because her father wanted her to become a professional: "My dad said why don't you try doing these and then you can become a doctor or pharmacist, the typical Asian subjects, but I don't know why I did those in A-levels because they weren't my stronger subjects". Her father refused her the option of taking other routes, such as GNVQs. A-levels were his preferred route but this was to the detriment of Kalpana who found them extremely difficult. In her first year of Sixth Form, Kalpana studied Biology, Chemistry and Maths. She failed all three and retook her A-levels and this time was told to take Computing, Maths, Business Studies and General studies but again failed. She studied again at A-level and this time took Business Studies, Law, General Studies and AS-levels in Statistics and ICT. She managed to pass this time and finally got a place at Leeds Metropolitan University to study Information Communication Management. Her choice of degree infuriated her father, but she had learnt the lesson during the A-levels about attempting subjects she was incapable of passing. These kinds of situation may go some way to explaining why there are rather lower levels of attainment among Pakistani and Bangladeshi women at A-level. They may also go some way to explaining the difficulties that they face in gaining entrance to some universities that may not accept re-sits.

4

Experiences of university and beyond

In this chapter we look at some of the young women's experiences of university. We examine how the young women are financing their HE. Among those in the Sixth Form we discovered that this was an issue that they had not thought about in any detail. Among those currently at university and recent graduates we found varying levels of debt, and for the vast majority considerable reliance on parents and siblings for support both in cash and kind.

Some young women found the transition to university quite stressful as they were often moving from a situation at school where South Asian women were either a majority or a substantial minority to university where they were often a small minority. Most of the women we interviewed were also aware of the differences in status between different universities, but none would have ever considered applying to Oxford or Cambridge and those institutions were not felt to be for 'people like us'.

Finally, we consider the impact of HE on the young women. Here we found that many appreciated not just the intellectual opportunities that had been afforded by university, but also the chance for independence and personal development.

Financing their degrees

Changes to the funding of students in the 1990s have reportedly had negative effects on widening participation (Callender, 2003; National Audit Office, 2002; Woodrow et al, 2002; Archer et al, 2004). At least one study has reported that South Asian Muslim students are the least likely to take out loans; just over half do so compared with 74% of White students and 66% of Black students. Such students were more likely to be living with their parents. Some have also speculated that Muslim students may refuse to take out loans for religious reasons (Callender and Kemp, 2000, p 77). Callender and Kemp also noted that working-class students were more likely to take out loans and to have debts of a higher value than middle-class students. The most recent study, in 2004-05, found that South Asian students had the lowest incomes of any ethnic group – £6,104 per annum compared with £8,531 for Black British students. More than half of South Asian students were living with parents – 58% compared with 16% of all students (Finch et al, 2006).

The debts of the current students and graduates who we interviewed ranged from zero to £18,000, with many of the young women reporting debts of between £9,000 and £10,000 regardless of religion or whether or not they were living away from home. They were not only owed to the Student Loans Company, but also included credit cards, bank overdrafts and loans from friends. The highest level of debt of £18,000 was reported by a Pakistani Muslim graduate living away from home.

Those in the Sixth Form seemed to be poorly informed about the financial demands of going to university and they had vague ideas about their own financial planning. Many assumed that there would be a combination of support from their parents, student loans and their own part-time employment. As Hajra Khan, a Pakistani Sixth Form student in Leeds, told us: "I know I have the support of my parents or probably student loan". In a very few instances Muslim Sixth Form students were opposed to taking out a loan on the grounds that they are *haram* (forbidden) in Islam. This was the reason given by Zarqa Aslam, a Bangladeshi Sixth Form student in Leeds: "'Cos at the end you'll have to pay it all back with interest added on it and in Islam we're not allowed to pay interest".

Many of the sixth-formers were currently in receipt of Education Maintenance Allowance (EMA), designed to help the children of low-income families continue into further education. For example, Rupreet Kaur, a Sikh student studying for GNVQs at a further education college in Birmingham told us: "I get EMA, that's £30 a week the money I get for college". EMAs seemed to be a significant source of financial support, easing the strain on family resources as the young women studied for the necessary A-level or GNVQs required for entry to university degrees.

Most of the current undergraduates and recent graduates drew on a 'mixed economy' of financial support for their HE from loans, parents and siblings and their own employment. In this respect they were very like other undergraduates (Finch et al, 2006), except many were relying on more parental support. Direct financial support from parents and even the wider family was especially important for almost all of the current undergraduates, and this may be creating new layers of obligation and dependence between parents and their offspring. There was little aversion to the necessity of using student loans. Refusal to take out loans was found to a limited extent among a few Muslim students, but among Sikh and Hindu students it also existed, based on the negative experiences of older siblings and the advice of parents. Finally, despite the strong desire to pursue further qualifications, the self-financing of postgraduate qualifications was especially difficult. This last feature is likely to be a significant source of further educational inequality in the future as many more people graduate with first degrees.

The financial strategies of the current undergraduates and recent graduates who we interviewed can be classified as follows:

- mixed economy of loans, wages and parental support;
- rejection of loans due to religious objections or risk;
- using loans as an insurance;
- dependence on parents;
- independence from parents;
- support from siblings and the extended family;
- state benefits.

Mixed economy of loans, wages and parental support

The mixed economy model was most typical, yet it was most likely to be found among those Indian students who were living way from home. We suspect that they were most like the stereotypical White middle-class student at a Russell Group university:

> 'I've got a loan and my parents help me out a lot. My parents pay my course fees and then I use my loan to live off and my wages. Usually every term they'll give me a lump sum to help me out.' (Davinder Kaur, Indian undergraduate, Leeds)

Rejection of loans due to religious objections or risk

Only a minority of the current undergraduates expressed an aversion to taking out loans. Only a few Muslim students did not take out loans because they are *haram*. Many of these students received additional support from their parents for this reason:

> 'We didn't take out a loan as it had interest on it and in Islam interest is forbidden so there was no point getting something and you have to pay back with interest at the end so whatever happens my mum and dad said 'we'll help you out'.' (Rahila Akhtar, Indian Muslim graduate, Leeds)

Other students told us that they avoided debt because of the negative experiences of older siblings. This also indicated how parents often felt obliged to help in order for their daughters to avoid debt. It does seem then that the newer systems of student finance are creating whole new relationships of obligation and dependence between parents and children as parents help their younger children after seeing the older siblings get into serious debt:

> 'My brother took out a loan, he's got over £21,000 debt, he's only just got married, Sadia my eldest sister only took out a loan twice for two fees – she was in £7k debt. She's got a job now so she can begin to pay it back. My mum was like "You are not going through that", and my sister was "No we are not having you in debt, if you need any money I will support you".' (Bushra Kauser, Indian undergraduate, Birmingham)

Using loans as an insurance

Another strategy for financial management was to obtain a student loan, but not to draw down the money except in times of exceptional need. This was particularly found among Muslim students due to their aversion to getting into debt. They would have preferred not to have to take out loans as they are seen as *haram*, but treated them as an insurance that most found they had to draw on at some point. Shazia Begum, a Bangladeshi undergraduate in Leeds, explained to us that: "I have taken out a loan but I haven't used it. It's in case if I might need it or something or need extra money."

Dependence on parents

There were a few instances where parents maintained control over their daughters' finances. In these cases some young women had ceased using credit cards, and had followed their parents' advice about loans and savings:

> 'I'm not good with handling money you know. I've had all my credit cards taken off me so I only get cash now. So until I can prove to my dad that I can spend wisely am not allowed to have one.… It's so embarrassing, I'm 20 but I still get spending money off my dad. I work weekends and I only get £80-£90 a week so I don't spend that, it goes in an account for the future.' (Beenish Kaur, Indian undergraduate, Birmingham)

Independence from parents

One other financial strategy was to seek total financial independence from parents. This was often done through working while studying, and was motivated by a desire for autonomy from the family and self-reliance. However, this autonomy carried the price of increased levels of debt:

'Financially I didn't accept a penny off my parents. I refused. I wouldn't take any money off my brothers or off my parents. I fought them every step of the way. And I think that for me was really important because I needed to know that I was independent and that I was doing it on my own. Not 'cos I want to be able to say I've done it on my own but just to be able to know that I can.' (Samreen Patel, Pakistani graduate, Leeds)

Support from siblings and the extended family

Although almost all of the young women who we interviewed reported some kind of parental support, some told us that their husbands, brothers and sisters were also providing support. In some cases the support from siblings seemed to be especially important. In these cases the whole financial resources of the wider extended family are mobilised to support the education of the young woman, which demonstrates that the families' and the wider community's commitment to the university education of the daughters is very substantial indeed:

'Whenever I am going home my brother is always giving me money and recently I've been short of money so he gives me an allowance of about £50 per week, which is fine by me. He has supported me a lot, when I'm short of paying my rent and stuff he pays.' (Jameela Yaqoob, Bangladeshi undergraduate, Leeds)

State benefits

A few students relied on state benefits to support themselves during their education. These were young mothers, sometimes divorced from their husbands. Zoreena Bibi, who started her degree when she was aged 24, explained how she had relied on state benefits during her time at university as a mother:

'I financed my degree because I was on Income Support, 80% of the fees were paid and 20% I paid, which wasn't much, and the second degree – the postgraduate – I had to finance it fully. It was a struggle, but I looked for funding but they said studying for a higher education like masters is a privilege you should be able to finance it yourself.' (Zoreena Bibi, Bangladeshi graduate, Leeds)

Being in a 'mixed' environment

Within Leeds there were considerable differences in the experiences of students attending the University of Leeds and Leeds Metropolitan University, in terms of race and ethnicity. Those studying at the University of Leeds found themselves within a predominantly White environment, whereas those within Leeds Metropolitan University experienced more of an ethnically mixed institution. Table A11 in the Appendix gives details of the ethnic composition of the student bodies in those institutions that most of our interviewees attended. While these show little difference between the two main universities in Leeds, the concentration of South Asian students in particular courses at Leeds Metropolitan University as well as that university's positive image among minority ethnic groups affected those students' experiences in a positive way.

The tendency to study at home, which appears to be most pronounced among South Asian female undergraduates, is thought by some of the widening participation and careers service officers to be producing a different experience of university. They felt that such students were becoming isolated because they did not live in residences with other students, and were merely at university between 9am and 5pm. As a result, some institutions had begun rethinking the character of their 'freshers week' to reflect these changes among students. There was the perception that South Asian female undergraduates were not part of 'university life' as it is traditionally seen for White undergraduates:

> 'I think a lot of it is about social isolation generally if you're living at home and not having those networks and the social side of education so we hope that we are having student peer support, if anyone is having difficulties we'll be able to identify those issues early on and they'll feel more integrated more quickly.' (Careers service officer, AE)

However, South Asian women were able to form strong friendships and support networks with other South Asian women on campus. For them the issue was the very small numbers of South Asian people on their courses compared with their experiences of school and Sixth Form. Students sometimes experienced a sense of surprise or shock in the first instance as they noted that there were so few South Asian people at their university compared with the schools and Sixth Forms. Some were often the only students from their backgrounds on their courses and this was particularly isolating. Many maintained strong friendships with other South Asian women and for some these were an especially strong source of support in overwhelmingly White environments.

For those at the University of Leeds, the transition from schools with significant numbers of minority ethnic pupils to an overwhelmingly White environment has an impact. For instance, according to Isha Sharma, an Indian undergraduate, "I wasn't used to seeing so many White people in one area!" Jameela Yaqoob, a Bangladeshi Muslim, reiterated such sentiments: "When I first came to Uni I thought, oh my god, where are all the Asians? I couldn't see any Asians, and my courses especially and I was thinking, where the hell are they?"

But for some of the women the issue of ethnic difference was raised for them by the reactions of the White people they encountered who had sometimes never personally known South Asian people before, and brought certain stereotypes with them. Some of their fellow White students assumed that all South Asian women do not drink and socialise in the same way as young White people. They had a stereotype of the 'typical Indian girl' as domesticated and compliant:

> 'When I interact with people I don't think I'm a brown girl and you're a white man, but it was other people that made me aware. It was like "Wow, look at you, I've never met an Indian person before." I said "I can't be a representative for all Indian people. I'm one experience of it." They said "Wow, but you go out drinking, you're not typical." I said "How can you say that, what is a typical Indian girl?" They had this image of a girl that stands in the kitchen.' (Davinder Kaur, Indian undergraduate, Leeds)

Some South Asian women had relatively few South Asian friends prior to coming to university. However, now in an environment that is predominately White, paradoxically they have far more contact with other South Asian students. As a result they learn more about their South Asian roots and the diversity among South Asians:

'At home I have two Indian friends, the rest are all White. In contrast to here no one can believe I live with four Indian women here! We are so different … we have been to each others family homes for 21st birthdays … you think, wow, we are all Indian, but we are all so different!' (Simi Banu, Indian undergraduate, Leeds)

However, in other cases the young women decided to detach themselves from those who were not of the same ethnic background. In these cases a common ethnic and religious identity, shared experiences and understandings seemed to provide these students with an important sources of support in the 'White social space' of the university:

'Most of my social circle is in the Asian community, I mean I can speak to my White friends up until certain point … there is more of common understanding between you and your Asian friend. You talk about things that are a bit more deeper and your friendship is more deeper because you feel as though they understand you … I don't want to make more White friends but I do have White friends.' (Fatima Begum, Bangladeshi undergraduate, Leeds)

In a similar way, the ethnic composition of particular degree courses may be more important than the ethnic composition of the whole university's student body. While there may be a 'critical mass' of South Asian students at the level of the whole institution, on a day-to-day basis students experience life in the lectures and seminars of their own degree course. For example, Saima Mamood, a Pakistani graduate, found it hard being the only Asian girl on her course: "The school I went to was predominately Asian, and, I mean, you go from one extreme to another".

Experiences of racism in public places, schools and at university

The young women who we interviewed described experiences of racism directed towards them in public places, at school from staff and students and at university from staff and students. The forms of racist behaviours varied from physical attacks to cultural assumptions, especially about the gendered character of South Asian culture. Much of the racism was also in the form of Islamophobia, and even many non-Muslim students experienced this as many White non-Muslims apparently assumed all South Asians were Muslims. While none of the women said that they had complained formally to their universities, those who had complained at school or college said they had been ignored. The racism in universities seemed to be most frequently encountered in those institutions and courses with very small numbers of minority ethnic students.

Many of the women who we interviewed talked about experiencing verbal comments from White men, and much of this explicit verbal racism was in public places, workplaces and where the young women lived. As clothing is often seen as an ethnic marker for many South Asian women, those who wore headscarves (*hijab*) tended to experience the most explicit and extreme forms racism:

'Once where I worked as a receptionist I was wearing *hijab*. They just assumed I couldn't read, it was sort of like reading a notice in front of me and they were just slowly reading it … so they think you're backward if you wear a *hijab*. (Zoreena Bibi, Bangladeshi graduate, Leeds)

The Bangladeshi and Indian women talked about being called 'Pakis', especially when they had been at school or in public spaces. The label 'Paki' to the women meant 'Pakistani'. As Jameela Yaqoob, a Bangladeshis undergraduate commented: "I've been called 'Paki', but you think 'well, I'm not a Paki, so why are you calling me a Paki?' They seem to call everyone a 'Paki'." The Bangladeshi and Indian women took most offence to this particular type of racist name-calling.

The interviewing took place after the 2001 September 11 attacks in the US, and some of the women had suffered from the backlash of September 11, in particular those wearing the *hijab*. For others a lot of questions were being asked at school or university after the September 11 attacks. This demonstrates very vividly that educational institutions are not insulated from wider events that may provoke racist incidents. The events of 2001 have thus added further public pressure on individual Muslim students to justify and defend their faith and identity when interacting with non-Muslims in educational institutions:

> 'There's always that kind of tension of always being put on the spot and always being made to feel like you have to clarify your position that you disagree with the terrorists and all that kind of thing. I mean you're made to feel like an outsider in terms of you're always being told to condemn terrorism even though you shouldn't have to, obviously it goes against what you believe, I think particularly my Muslim identity that's where I feel its always being questioned.' (Shahida Azam, Indian Muslim undergraduate, Leeds)

In relation to their experiences at school the young women talked about the stereotypes that some teachers had of them. These assumptions in some cases were seen as being buttressed by the public comments of some prominent local politicians, again illustrating the ways in which schools and universities are not insulated from the outside world:

> 'I have heard of cases where a lot of teachers still think that a lot of Asian women are not being allowed onto further studies and that as soon as they turn 16 they are shipped off to Pakistan to get married. Most of this stuff is fomented by our local MP, Ann Cryer; she made many comments on how women should not be getting married until they have gone on to university and things, and these comments are aimed at the Pakistanis and Bangladeshis.' (Tahira Safder, Pakistani graduate, Leeds)

The women were very critical of some staff in schools who had shown a lack of interest in South Asian pupils. Many of the women who we interviewed had either encountered or heard about teachers who did not take the education of South Asian women seriously. This seemed to especially apply to Bangladeshi and Pakistani women and to working-class Indian (often Sikh) students. This minority of teachers assumed, often quite openly, that South Asian women's education was going to be a waste of time as they were only destined for marriage and motherhood rather than for careers. This was felt to carry rather demeaning assumptions about motherhood as well as South Asians:

> 'At school I just felt like some teachers didn't want to teach me because I was Asian, and I was a stereotyped as an Asian. The teachers felt that we weren't interested in education and we didn't want to learn anything or we were a waste of time. I had one teacher who told me that I was fake basically, and just things like that – you see certain teachers, predominantly White, target Asian people.' (Jasvinder Kaur, Sikh undergraduate, Leeds)

While at school or Sixth Form College some women had taken up their dissatisfaction with the attitudes of some teachers, but in all the cases that we were told about this had been to no avail:

> 'He had this idea in his head that we as Asian women, our parents wouldn't allow us to go to Uni, and he was just wasting his time teaching us. We spoke to the head of year and he just said "Look, I'm stuck here, this man leaves college and

I've got a whole class that I have no teacher for." It was a really bad situation but the thing is, even though it was a really bad thing at the time, it was really distressing and really upsetting.' (Parveen Ali, Pakistani graduate, Leeds)

Some of the women felt that they suffered from racism within the education environment from fellow students that was also ignored by teaching staff. When they raised the matter with teachers they found that the teachers were reluctant to intervene, leaving them to deal with the situation themselves:

'They didn't like the way we dressed and everything and they just started criticising every little thing we did so we told the teachers about it and they didn't do nothing about it....' (Nalufa Begum, Bangladeshi sixth-former, Leeds)

At university the racism experienced by young South Asian women also came from fellow students as well as from staff. For the most part this was often in the form of unacknowledged assumptions about young South Asian women. These often revolved around what might be termed liberal stereotypes about oppressed South Asian women, especially Muslim women. Some felt that they were constantly having to correct White liberal myths about South Asian Muslim women that they felt at root were both racist and sexist in their failure to appreciate the change and diversity in South Asian communities:

'Talking to students they were like asking questions: "Is your mum allowing you to come and study?" "Is your husband all right about it?" Yeah, there are myths ... you just have to tell them things are changing and put them right.' (Zoreena Bibi, Bangladeshi graduate, Leeds)

Assumptions about Islam and Muslims also crept into the teaching context in those subjects where issues around the relationship between Islam and 'the West' were encountered. In one case the Muslim students in the lecture felt uncomfortable about the way the topic was treated by the lecturer:

'... one of my lecturers whilst giving a lecture on enlightenment and stuff it made me and a few of my other Muslim friends we kind of felt that we are being discriminated against, and that he didn't really like Muslims. That's one time when I felt a bit scared that a lecturer is trying to put his personal views across when he should have been objective.' (Zainab Ali, Bangaldeshi graduate, Leeds)

Some others told us of quite explicit comments or actions from a few academic staff that questioned their academic ability. Samreen Patel, a Pakistani graduate who had gone on to successfully complete a PhD, told us of her experience in a department that had few British minority ethnic students as undergraduates, but many international students at postgraduate level: "When I was doing my MA I had a lecturer here in the [x] department, who when I told him I was going to do a PhD laughed in my face".

Among the young women who had graduated many were finding it difficult to obtain graduate-level jobs, a phenomenon recently highlighted by the Equal Opportunities Commission (EOC, 2006). While we did not specifically ask about racism in postgraduate employment in detail, some of the graduates did tell us about experiences of racism after graduation in response to our general questions about their experiences of racism. These often combined racist and sexist assumptions. Parveen Ali, for example, had problems getting a training contract after she had qualified as a solicitor. Even when she did obtain a place with a firm of South Asian male solicitors, it was not quite what she was expecting:

'I just found it really, really difficult, being an Asian female to find a training contract. I know it sounds like a silly thing to say, but people just look at you differently, because they think, "God, what she's twenty-something now, she's obviously going to get married soon, then she's going to have kids, is it worth us investing the money that we're going to have to invest in getting her to qualify as a solicitor, the next thing you know, she'll be taking maternity leave, do we really want to go down that road?" Then I started working at a criminal law practice initially, in Leeds, for a group of Asian men, who had just set up a criminal law practice. I started working for them, and it wasn't quite what I expected it to be. I think they took advantage of the fact that I was Asian, that I was female and I was making far too many cups of tea, etc, so I left.' (Parveen Ali, Pakistani graduate, Leeds)

Those graduates who were considering academic careers were discouraged by what they were told about racism and sexism in academic life. For example, Samreen Patel, the Pakistani graduate mentioned above who had completed her PhD, was told by one of her White male academic mentors:

'He said you shouldn't go for a career in academia because you'll never be a professor because no Asian woman will ever become a professor in this country. You know at which point I thought, that's it, I have to, you know, how dare I not be a professor and now I have to. I'm not sure that I want to be now.' (Samreen Patel, Pakistani graduate, Leeds)

While much of the recent focus on racism in universities has been on institutional racism imbued in their culture and routines (Law et al, 2004), we have documented evidence of South Asian women's experience of racism at the interpersonal level inside and outside educational establishments. This acts as a further barrier towards their educational and career success. Within universities experiences of racism seemed more likely to occur in those institutions or departments with relatively low numbers of minority ethnic students. Further research would be necessary to confirm this finding. Furthermore, the forms of racism experienced often combined assumptions about both gender and the culture of British South Asian communities. In addition, much of the racism experienced was really Islamophobia directed at both Muslim and non-Muslim students.

Perceptions of different universities

Widening participation and careers service officers felt that there was a strong tendency for South Asian women to apply to 'former polytechnics' or 'new universities'. However, there were two views about this issue. One perspective emphasised the way in which universities are becoming ethnically marked as either largely for the White and middle class or more welcoming to minority ethnic students. In the West Midlands, for example, one widening participation officer (SC) told us: "… anecdotally teachers will say that certain communities see UCE [University of Central England] as their university of choice because of feeling that that would be a more comfortable institution for them to be in."

In contrast, others saw the issue in terms of the kinds of courses on offer and the grades required for entry. These were seen as being especially attractive to those who were in the first generation to go to university:

'… that's not to suggest that our students have got lower grades but in some cases that is the case. Again there is this issue of first generation in higher education. So that the part of the Widening Participation group, some of them were local to a fairly large Asian population. One of three institutions that have lower entry points, vocational courses….' (Careers officer, PM)

However, the young women who we interviewed saw differences between universities in terms of prestige. They readily pointed out differences between the two main universities within Leeds as they did within Birmingham. Within Leeds the women acknowledged the higher status that the University of Leeds has in comparison to Leeds Metropolitan University. For instance, Aaliyah went to the University of Leeds because of its reputation: "I heard everyone saying it's such a good Uni, and it's quite well known and everything". Besides suggestions about the institution in terms of its course, the women went on to distinguish between the academic level of the students. For example, Jasmin Ali studies Law at Leeds Metropolitan University, and noted the difference between getting a Law degree from there and from the University of Leeds: "In the Met people are not really as clever as people that go to Uni". The women interviewed at Leeds Metropolitan University had lower expectations of their A-level grades and therefore applied to former polytechnics or 'new universities' as they did not think they were going to get the grades to get into 'old universities', confirming the views of widening participation officers.

In terms of those students currently at university, there was huge significance placed on the prestige of a university in the vast majority of instances. All the women at the University of Leeds, for example, had applied because of its reputation of being a good university, even those who were living at home with their parents. Even the women who studied at Leeds Metropolitan University acknowledged the difference between them. They also acknowledged the differences in job prospects, as they perceived employers as being more interested in students who had attended 'old universities' such as the University of Leeds. Despite this widespread knowledge of the varying prestige of institutions, we did not encounter anyone who had applied to Oxford or Cambridge, and none had even considered doing so. They were felt to be totally 'out of their league'.

University and beyond

Experience of university life and HE changed the women's perceptions of many issues. They felt that they now saw things differently after their education at university, as well as noting the more explicit intellectual and personal development. They reported being more able to 'tolerate' their own communities, as well as learning about other communities. One result of going to university was to have re-evaluated their own relationship to their own community:

> 'There was no way I was going to work with my community because I had a certain arrogance about my community, well now I am working with the community I am less judgemental because … I have become less ignorant, I would say.' (Amina Chowdhury, Bangladeshi graduate, Leeds)

Together with an increased sense of their own autonomy and self-confidence, university was for many of the women an empowering as well as an intellectually challenging experience. One particular contrast was between the uncertainty and lack of confidence among the sixth-formers compared with the sense of empowerment and self-confidence among those who had graduated.

While boosting confidence, the women also found the experience of university enlightening intellectually. Some of the women who had graduated recently described to us how they felt optimistic about their futures with dreams of upward social mobility. For example, Sobia Ali, a Bangladeshi graduate, told us that: "In terms of my CV it looks a lot better and in terms of knowledge, being aware of the outside world and issues, so yes I'm in tune with things".

Among those who had moved away from the family home to go to university, the women who were in their final year discussed the possibility of returning home again. Although the women talked about a positive relationship with their parents, they felt that if they went back home they would lose their independence and the self-reliance they had discovered living on their own. They also felt that their parents and families would still think they were the same people they were before they went to university:

> 'I'm finding it hard moving back home because I've not lived at home for five years now and I'm really worried about it. I love going home … but living there is such a different experience. It's like going back to being a teenager and I'm really scared about it.' (Davinder Kaur, Indian undergraduate, Leeds)

5

South Asian women, widening participation and careers

In this chapter we consider the perspectives of widening participation and careers service professionals in universities. We examine what use is made of the careers services in particular by South Asian women, and what kinds of issues they raised with university careers service staff. Such staff tended to be reluctant to generalise, but they did recall some issues that had been raised. For example, these often concerned marriage and the preferences among parents for certain subjects and careers for their daughters: "Well, families, parents, people reluctant to encourage their daughters to go into higher education or to any environment such as higher education" (Careers officer, PM).

In relation to future employment there was some especially innovative work among the various careers services, such as those addressing the specific problems that Muslim students who wore the *hijab* may face. These initiatives involved arranging discussions between employers and students around this question. For instance, students had expressed concerns about how to approach job interviews:

> 'We've had a lot of students that have had issues with things like wearing *hijab*, and how they've dealt with that. We've had employers trying to address those issues with students as well.' (Careers officer, LH)

Perspectives on how far South Asian female students were interested in further training and postgraduate courses varied among the careers service staff. In some cases in those universities where most students were pursuing 'vocational' qualifications it was felt that there was little interest in further qualifications as their undergraduate degrees prepared them for direct entry to the labour market. However, there were suggestions that some South Asian women were pursuing postgraduate qualifications to further delay marriage:

> 'Yes, I would say that quite a few are going into postgraduate courses … and a lot of these students have said to me, "I fancy doing a Masters", and like I say, you challenge it as to why they do want to do a Masters, and it's because they're trying to get away from something that is perhaps family based…. Students have been very, very honest with me, because it's not like they've been hinting at these things, they've stated it quite blatantly.' (Careers officer, LH)

A key question is how far institutions identify South Asian women for widening participation and careers service initiatives. In most instances there was nothing being attempted that specifically targets South Asian women. In other cases, however, institutions had set up 'summer schools' for South Asian girls from local Sixth Forms who were considering university:

'Targeting those groups … we have various summer schools, some of which
– well, there's an Asian Women's Summer School for example.… But unfortunately
it can only work with relatively small number of schools, in a wider region – it isn't
just Leeds.' (Careers officer, PM)

Some widening participation officers felt that some South Asian girls were only interested
in 'traditional' professions such as Medicine and Law, and were deterred by the realisation
that high A-level scores as well as considerable finance is needed to pursue these
qualifications. This suggests that there is a considerable amount of work to be done in
outlining the alternative qualifications and careers for those young South Asian women
considering going to university. In some instances widening participation officers saw these
sometimes unrealistic career plans as arising from family expectations:

'… it is about expectation within the family of what is kind of acceptable, if you
like, reason to go to university and if you're going to go to university it's because
you're going to get a very good job which translates to being a doctor or a lawyer.'
(Widening participation officer, SC)

This was also reflected in some of the young women's views, as discussed above.

Barriers to successful widening participation and careers service work

A number of important barriers to the improvement of widening participation and careers
services for South Asian women emerged from the research. In some instances widening
participation officers faced difficulties in their contacts with schools. In other cases
initiatives failed because those working on them did not have the right contacts in the
communities they were attempting to reach. This underlines the importance of having the
right staff or the right community contacts – in terms of both ethnicity and gender – for
this kind of work. As one widening participation officer recalled about a project in her
institution that failed:

'I guess it was because we didn't have the right contacts. The contacts we had
with those groups were with men. So actually getting through to, for example,
Bangladeshi women.' (Widening participation officer, SC)

More generally it was felt that the Connexions Service has not been serving this particular
group of students very well. The Connexions Service was felt to be serving the most
deprived or excluded groups. Consequently, many Bangladeshi and Pakistani women
who are first generation entrants to HE are being neglected, as their schools often lack
the expertise or resources to advise them adequately about their HE choices and their
subsequent careers and they do not fall into the groups served by the Connexions Service.
Bangladeshi and Pakistani women who are most likely to be considering university are
very likely to have five good GCSEs and such young people are not a priority for the
Connexions Service:

'The Connexions Service are the people who now deliver careers guidance in
schools. The way in which that is structured, they target the lower-level social
groups, and so the middle-class groups … don't get a service. The view is they're
smart enough to make decisions and plan out the options themselves, which
perhaps isn't the case. On the contrary, they've got more choice than some of the
other kids who are less able, but the focus of attention has always been on the
socially disadvantaged through Connexions, and that's a political thing nationally.'
(Careers officer, PM)

One widening participation officer went on to describe how initiatives from within the university sector are channelling resources to try and address this gap. These concerns were expressed in both West Yorkshire and the West Midlands:

'I guess that's one thing that Aim Higher is also trying to address in looking at progression routes for vocational learners and more information about higher education. We try and fulfil that role as well to some extent to our mentors and tutors that they are our resource to talk about higher education and teachers can use them to do that.' (Widening participation officer, AE)

Throughout the research we found that those instances of both widening participation projects and careers guidance projects aimed either directly at South Asian women, or indirectly because they were part of some other target group such as first generation entrants to HE, were reliant on short-term funding. This carries the considerable risk that much of the knowledge, skill and contacts developed as part of these programmes are being lost as the funding ends and those employed on the projects move. Nevertheless, many senior staff in these services did seem to be committed to trying to retain these activities:

'The fixed term reflects the nature of the funding and that's the unfortunate element but I know they are looking into mainstream and we're about to put a case to our academic board which will actually give continuity to this kind of activity.' (Widening participation officer, AE)

This desire to 'mainstream' such activities also applies to the careers service often in recognition of the specific problems facing minority ethnic graduates in the labour market. University careers services have also in recent years been developing projects to work with groups such as South Asian women. This underlines a particularly important point, namely that despite graduating, South Asian women remain disadvantaged in the labour market, as is discussed in more detail above. As one university careers service employee told us:

'I'm hoping we can mainstream it, but the sort of figures that I showed you, we used figures like that, not the particular ones you've got there, to show that there is a need, that minority ethnic learners are still disadvantaged in the labour market and that's the national picture as the local picture and that we really ought to do something about it.' (Careers service officer, PM)

In some instances innovative projects aimed at South Asian women, especially those from a Bangladeshi or Pakistani background, fail to obtain funding. This might be because South Asians are still treated in some circles as a single homogenous and successful group, thereby overlooking the position of Muslims for example, and the difficult labour market position that many South Asian women with degrees find themselves in (EOC, 2006). For example, we were told of case where:

'In terms of Asian women we began to write a bid for the National Aiming Higher project working with city college, I don't know if you know it but they've got the women's academy and they do a lot of work with Asian women and we were hoping to do a joint project particularly looking at the issues with providing residential experiences. It then grew into working with parents and families but that didn't seem to get any mileage in it.' (Widening participation officer, SC)

We also uncovered some evidence that some of the promotional material for the recruitment of undergraduates featuring South Asian students would be misleading as in some institutions they would be in a small minority. In these cases institutions should be careful as to the impressions they would be giving potential minority ethnic students.

The reality may not live up to the image, as we found in our interviews with the young women: the 'Whiteness' of some universities was experienced as a shock and a source of strain. As one South Asian widening participation officer told us:

> 'Yes, they do put pictures of us in brochures. They've put in pictures of a Black girl and a Black guy and they've got a picture of an Asian girl with a headscarf on the website. And that's making it look like, yes, we do recruit … I think the girls that do come here that are practising Muslims or even just Indian or Sikh people, when they come here they'll get a shock because they'll be thinking it will be like a certain way, but it's not. There's not many Asian people here so they'll feel a bit isolated.' (Widening participation officer, IH)

Suggestions for improvements to services

Among widening participation officers a number of suggestions for improvement were raised. Some are specific to South Asian women, and others of more general applicability. For instance, one issue they see as important is that of retention of students once they arrive at university. They feel that currently very little work is being done in their institutions on this issue:

> 'It's almost like there's no focus on retention … nobody seems to think about the consequences of those students coming in and their retention and the support while they're here so that they do get to the end of the degree and actually get a good job....' (Widening participation officer, LH)

More specific themes concerning South Asian students include taking full advantage of their language skills. Many South Asian students are fluent in at least one South Asian language such as Bengali, Hindi or Punjabi. Some widening participation and careers staff are of the view that schools and universities could be making more of these skills that placed many South Asian students in an advantageous position compared with the majority of White students. For example, one widening participation officer told us:

> 'I felt that very few schools were really stressing to the pupils from the ethnic minorities with a multilingual background, that they were actually really so much ahead of the game in the fact that they had actually been brought up bilingually or trilingually … that actually they were really well placed to be extremely good linguists and were missing out on lots of tricks there.' (Careers service officer, AB)

There were different views about the advisability of employing South Asian female staff to deal specifically with the needs of South Asian female students as a way of improving services. However, without prompting, one White male head of a university careers service was adamant that this is one single thing he could do to improve his service for this group of students:

> 'I'd get an Asian female careers advisor if I possibly could but there aren't very many of those. I don't actually know any, well, I know one, and she works in London … but yes, that's the first thing I would do.' (Head of careers service, PM)

However, others were more sceptical of such an approach, taking the view that the services should be accessible to anyone, so that the employment of staff of a particular sex or ethnic background is unnecessary. Nevertheless, one Muslim woman working as an advisor at another institution was quite clear about the sense of identification that some students felt with her because she is a Muslim woman:

'I'm not South Asian but I'm a Muslim, you know it's quite easy for me to talk to them about issues relating to religion and culture and I'm able to talk to them, being very, very open with them as well you know like today we had one student who was wearing *hijab* and she been for interview and she herself said 'What do I do, do I shake hands with them' and that sort of thing. I can discuss a lot more in detail and I'm able in comparison with my other colleagues to be quite direct with them....' (Careers service officer, RC)

Ideas for improvements to widening participation and recruitment work included developing links with the communities and producing material for some parents in different languages. In one West Midlands institution they had produced materials in minority languages, but had not made much use of them in practice. One South Asian widening participation worker emphasised how easy it should be for institutions to develop links with their local South Asian communities:

'So improving the links, definitely going into the community and making yourself known. That is something they can achieve because like you said, going to Mela's and producing leaflets in different languages, any kind of event that is going on; be there, have a stand – it's not that hard you know.' (Widening participation officer, IH)

6

Conclusions: issues for policy, practice and future research

South Asian women of Pakistani and Bangladeshi origin remain among the lowest paid in the workforce. There continues to be increasing demand for HE among South Asian women. Their attainment at school has improved dramatically since the 1980s, especially among Bangladeshi and Pakistani women, and continues to do so. For a large minority of students changes in their lifestyle and independence are important reasons for going to university. They experience university generally as providing a sense of independence as well as the more explicit academic qualifications. Despite these ongoing successes there are still areas of concern. This research has highlighted four areas where policy and practice can start to address the barriers to university entrance and later success: broadening subject choice; improving widening participation and careers service work with South Asian women; improving the university experience for such women; and increasing the focus placed on future careers.

Broadening subject choice

South Asian women applying to university continue to be concentrated in subjects leading to 'traditional' professional careers or those with a strong 'vocational' element. Some of these, such as Law and Medicine, require very high A-level grades and there is intense competition for places, meaning that applicants face a lower chance of gaining entry. This focus on applying for these subjects is compounded by the fact that South Asian women at university are much less likely than White women to have come from a 'middle-class' background. Furthermore, they are less likely to have the highest A-level results.

One possible response to this is for local communities to recognise the value of a wider range of degree subjects that young women could be encouraged to apply for. Better provision of information about the range of career opportunities available for all graduates and not just those with professional or vocationally oriented degrees would enable a better fit between students and degree subjects, and should be provided to both students and their parents as part of widening participation activities. One obvious example is that you do not need a degree in Law to train for the Legal Practice Course that qualifies you as a solicitor.

For some of those studying for A-levels, especially those from Bangladeshi and Pakistani backgrounds, their decisions about education are being influenced by their impending marriage. This may well interrupt preparation for HE. For many are also restricted to local HE markets due to parental influences upon whether or not they leave home to study. This often limits their choice of university and type of course. It also disadvantages them in terms of work placements and their later career prospects.

However, this is a rapidly changing situation, with various forms of negotiated marriage becoming dominant. One possible response to the existence of local HE markets is for universities to ensure that a broad range of degree courses continues to be available locally. This would give such students a genuine choice of degree subject and would also benefit other students who have to study locally for other reasons. More universities should consider more local market research for their degree programmes, as there may be unmet demand for some subjects from local South Asian communities.

Young women's parents also often influence the choice of A-levels and degree subjects. Parents often show a strong preference for qualifications leading to careers in the traditional professions such as Law or Medicine, even when their daughters are relatively weak in these academic fields. In some case this may lead to failure and re-sits at A-level.

One policy and practice response to this issue is for university widening participation activities to point out the alternatives. There is also an important need for all of those involved in education at this level to make it clear that re-sits may disadvantage students. Another response is for university admissions tutors to reconsider their treatment of A-level re-sits. Further research into this area would clarify how widespread the differential treatment of re-sits really is.

Improving widening participation and careers service work

There are a range of obstacles and barriers to the work of widening participation and careers service staff with South Asian women. First there seem to be gaps left by the Connexions Service that provides careers advice for young people. As the Connexions Service is reorganised this gap should be explicitly addressed. In addition, the short-term funding of widening participation and careers service projects aimed at South Asian women and other disadvantaged groups of students means that projects are often too short to have any real effect. Furthermore, the short period of funding means that skilled staff and accumulated knowledge and experience are quickly lost. Poor contacts with minority ethnic communities also limit the ability of widening participation initiatives to be really effective. This is something that could be addressed by the Higher Education Funding Council for England since it provides the funding for such projects. As widening participation is a central goal of the current government, some more permanent or longer-term arrangements for such funding seems necessary to achieve sustained impact.

There seem to be very few widening participation initiatives aimed specifically at South Asian women. The exceptions found in this study were due to the long-running commitment of certain institutions, or were relatively small-scale summer schools. There is a sense that South Asian women have been overlooked by many universities in this respect. A range of initiatives in this area could improve the situation of the young women, their communities and universities' own performance in terms of widening participation. Developing better links with local minority ethnic communities should be a priority, and this may include providing material in minority languages for some parents.

In some cases university careers services are adapting their activities to address the issues that a more religiously diverse student body raises. South Asian women raise some issues with careers staff concerned with marriage and other cultural issues that influence their career and postgraduate training decisions. Muslim students also raise issues around wearing the *hijab* to job interviews, and some careers services respond to this issue in a creative and responsive way by bringing together employers and students to discuss their concerns.

Recognising the changing social profile of the students attending a university and their changing cultural and religious needs is seen as important by those in the careers service. University careers service staff see a need to be continually innovative in how services are provided to students by listening to their needs and adapting to them.

Improving the university experience

Young women have very different experiences in predominantly White institutions and courses as opposed to those with large numbers of South Asian students. Those in predominantly White institutions or courses are more likely to feel isolated. Universities or courses with a 'critical mass' of minority ethnic students are experienced as more comfortable and welcoming places. Students on courses without a 'critical mass' of minority ethnic students are more likely to report experiences of racism from staff and other students. Based on some of these experiences there is still an urgent need for some schools, colleges and universities to ensure that equality and diversity policies are seen to be delivered on the ground by successfully challenging unacceptable behaviour from staff and students.

South Asian women are concentrated in certain universities and courses. Those from a Bangladeshi or Pakistani background especially apply to local universities due to parental preferences. Some institutions might be seen as preferable because they have 'critical mass' of minority ethnic students and are seen as more welcoming. Students also follow the advice of friends and relatives by applying to institutions that they attended. Furthermore, South Asian women apply to institutions offering more vocational degrees asking for lower A-level scores. They have strong perceptions of the distinction between 'high status' and 'low status' universities, and see places such as Oxford and Cambridge as simply unattainable.

Focusing on future careers

Our statistical analysis shows that South Asian women graduates, especially those from a Bangladeshi or Pakistani background are less likely than White women graduates to obtain professional and managerial jobs. Women from Bangladeshi and Pakistani backgrounds are more likely to be economically inactive or unemployed, but if they have degree-level qualifications they are much less likely to unemployed. Careers officers and the Bangladeshi and Pakistani young women feel that women's options for moving to find employment are limited by family obligations and that this is limiting their career options.

Consequently, there should be more concern within universities with retention and the future careers of South Asian women students. Employing South Asian women as staff in careers services and widening participation to provide culturally appropriate advice and to act as role models should be considered as one way of beginning to address this.

References

Abbas, T. (2004) *The Education of British South Asians*, London: Palgrave.

Afshar, H. (1994) 'Muslim women in West Yorkshire: growing up with real and imaginary values amidst conflicting views of self and society', in H. Afshar and M. Maynard (eds) *The Dynamics of Race and Gender*, London: Taylor & Francis, pp 127-47.

Ahmad, F. (2001) 'Modern traditions? British Muslim women and academic achievement', *Gender and Education*, vol 13, no 2, pp 137-52.

Ahmad, F. (2003) 'Still in progress? Methodological dilemmas, tensions and contradictions in theorizing South Asian Muslim women', in N. Puwar and P. Raghuram (eds) *South Asian Women in the Diaspora*, Oxford: Berg, pp 43-65.

Ahmad, F., Modood, T. and Lissenburgh, S. (2003) *South Asian Women and Employment in Britain: The Interaction of Gender and Ethnicity*, London: PSI.

Anwar, M. (1998) *Between Cultures*, London: Routledge.

Archer, L., Hutchings, M. and Ross, A. (2004) *Higher Education and Social Class: Issues of Exclusion and Inclusion*, London: RoutledgeFalmer.

Bhatti, G. (1999) *Asian Children at Home and at School: An Ethnographic Study*, London: Routledge.

Bhopal, K. (1997a) *Gender, Race and Patriarchy*, Aldershot: Ashgate.

Bhopal, K. (1997b) 'South Asian women within households: dowries, degradation and despair', *Women's Studies International Forum*, vol 20, no 4, pp 483-92.

Bhopal, K. (2000) 'South Asian women in East London: the impact of education', *European Journal of Women's Studies*, vol 7, no 1, pp 35-52.

Brah, A. (1993) *Cartographies of Diaspora: Contesting Identities*, London: Routledge.

Clark, K. and Drinkwater, D. (2005) 'Some preliminary findings on ethnic minority labour market activity using Controlled Access Microdata', *SARS Newsletter*, February.

Callender, C. (2003) *Attitudes to Debt: School Leavers and Further Education Students' Attitudes to Debt and their Impact on Participation in Higher Education*, London: Universities UK.

Callender, C. and Kemp, M. (2000) *Changing Student Finances: Income, Expenditure and the Take-up of Student Loans Among Full- and Part-time Higher Education Students in 1998/9*, DfES Research Report RR213, London: Department for Education and Employment.

Connor, H., Tyers, C., Modood, T. and Hillage, J. (2004) *Why the Difference? A Closer Look at Higher Education Minority Ethnic Students and Graduates*, DfES Research Report RR552, Nottingham: DfES Publications.

Dale A., Lindley, J. and Dex, S. (2006) 'A life-course perspective on ethnic differences in women's economic activity in Britain', *European Sociological Review*, vol 22, pp 323-37.

Dale, A., Shaheen, N., Kalra, V. and Fieldhouse, E. (2002) 'Routes into education and employment for young Pakistani and Bangladeshi women in the UK', *Ethnic and Racial Studies*, vol 25, no 6, pp 942-68.

DWP (Department of Work and Pensions) (2006) *Households Below Average Income 2004-05*, London: The Stationery Office.

EOC (Equal Opportunities Commission) (2006) *Moving On Up? Bangladeshi, Pakistani and Black Caribbean Women and Work*, Manchester: EOC.

Finch, S., Jones, A., Parfrement, J. and Cebulla, A. (2006) *Student Income and Expenditure Survey 2004/05*, DfES Research Report RR725, London: Department for Education and Employment.

Ghuman, P. (1994) *Coping with Two Cultures*, Bristol: Longdum.

HESA (Higher Education Statistics Agency) (2006) *Student Tables 1994/95-2004/05*, www.hesa.ac.uk

Joly, D. (1995) *Britannia's Crescent: Making a Place for Muslims in British Society*, Aldershot: Ashgate.

Jones, T. (1993) *Britain's Ethnic Minorities*, London: PSI.

Kalra, S. S. (1980) *Daughters of Tradition: Adolescent Sikh Girls and their Accommodation to Life in British Society*, London: Third World Publications.

Khanum, S. (1995) 'Education and the Muslim girl', in M. Blair, J. Holland and S. Sheldon (eds) *Identity and Diversity: Gender and the Experience of Education*, Clevedon: Multilingual Matters, pp 279-88.

Law, I., Phillips, D. and Turney, L. (eds) (2004) *Institutional Racism in Higher Education*, Stoke-on-Trent: Trentham Books.

Leslie, D. and Drinkwater, S. (1999) 'Staying on in full-time education: reasons for higher participation rates among ethnic minority males and females', *Economica*, vol 66, pp 63-77.

Lindley, J. K., Dale, A. and Dex, S. (2006) 'Ethnic differences in women's employment: the changing role of qualifications', *Oxford Economic Papers*, vol 58, no 2, pp 351-78.

Low Pay Commission (2005) *National Minimum Wage: Low Pay Commission Report 2005*, Cmd 6475, London: The Stationery Office.

McManus, I. C., Esmail, A. and Demetriou, M. (1998) 'Factors affecting likelihood of applicants being offered a place in medical schools in the United Kingdom in 1996 and 1997: a retrospective study', *British Medical Journal*, vol 317, pp 1111-7.

McManus, I. C., Richards, P., Winder, B. C., Sproston, K. A. and Styles, V. (1995) 'Medical school applicants from ethnic minority groups: identifying if and when they are disadvantaged', *British Medical Journal*, vol 310, pp 496-500.

Modood, T. and Shiner, M. (1994) *Ethnic Minorities and Higher Education: Why are there Different Rates of Entry?*, London: PSI.

Modood, T., Berthoud, R., Lakey, J., Nazroo, J., Smith, P., Virdee, S. and Beishon, S. (1997) *Diversity and Disadvantage: Fourth National Survey of Ethnic Minorities*, London: PSI.

National Audit Office (2002) *Widening Participation in Higher Education in England*, London: The Stationery Office.

Owen, C., Mortimore, P. and Phoenix, A. (1997) 'Higher education qualifications', in V. Karn (ed) *Ethnicity in the 1991 Census. Vol 4: Employment, Education and Housing among the Ethnic Minority Populations of Great Britain*, London: The Stationery Office, pp 1-16.

Peach, C. (2006) 'Muslims in the 2001 Census of England and Wales: gender and economic disadvantage', *Ethnic and Racial Studies*, vol 29, no 4, pp 629-55.

Penn, R. and Scattergood, H. (1992) 'Ethnicity and career aspirations in contemporary Britain', *New Community*, vol 19, no 1, pp 75-98.

Platt, L. (2002) *Parallel Lives? Poverty among Ethnic Minority Groups in Britain*, London: Child Poverty Action Group.

Platt, L. (2006) *Pay Gaps: The Position of Ethnic Minority Women and Men*, Manchester: Equal Opportunities Commission.

Reay, D., David, M. and Ball, S. (2005) *Degrees of Choice: Social Class, Race and Gender in Higher Education*, Stoke: Trentham Books.

Seth, S. (1985) 'Education of Asian women', in M. Hughes and M. Kennedy (eds) *New Futures: Changing Women's Education*, London: Routledge & Kegan Paul, pp 121-35.

Shaw, A. (1994) 'The Pakistani community in Oxford', in R. Ballard (ed) *Desh Pardesh: The South Asian Presence in Britain*, London: Hurst and Company, pp 35-57.

Shiner, M. and Modood, T. (2002) 'Help or hindrance? Higher education and the route to ethnic equality', *British Journal of Sociology of Education*, vol 23, no 2, pp 209-32.

Stopes-Roe, M. and Cochrane, R. (1990) *Citizens of This Country: The Asian British*, Clevedon: Multilingual Matters.

Tanna, K. (1990) 'Excellence, equality and educational reform: the myth of South Asian achievement levels', *New Community*, vol 16, no 3, pp 349-68.

Wade, B. and Souter, P. (1992) *Continuing To Think: The British Asian Girl*, Clevedon: Multilingual Matters.

Westwood, S. and Hoffman, D. (1979) *Asian Women: Education and Social Change*, Leicester: University of Leicester.

Wilson, A. (1978) *Finding a Voice*, London: Virago.

Woodrow, M., Yorke, M., Lee, M.F., McGrane, J., Osborne, B., Pudner, H. and Trotman, C. (2002) *Social Class and Participation*, London: Universities UK.

Appendix

Table A1: Summary of sample of interviewees

	Leeds				Birmingham			
	16-18	Under-graduate	Graduate	Total	16-18	Under-graduate	Graduate	Total
Bangladeshi	10	8	2	20	2	2	2	6
Indian	2	11	11	24	2	8	3	13
Pakistani	16	7	10	33	7	7	4	18
Total	28	26	23	77	11	17	9	37

Table A2: Women's economic activity rate by ethnic group and age, England and Wales, 2001 (%)

	White British	Indian	Pakistani	Bangladeshi
Aged 16-24				
Economically active	100.0	100.0	100.0	100.0
Employed part-time	13.5	10.8	17.2	18.4
Employed full-time	54.2	43.0	36.8	33.9
Self-employed part-time	0.4	0.3	0.6	0.3
Self-employed full-time	0.8	0.8	1.1	0.6
Unemployed	6.4	7.9	16.8	15.8
Student	24.8	37.1	27.5	30.9
Economically inactive	100.0	100.0	100.0	100.0
Retired	0.2	0.2	0.1	0.1
Student	67.3	80.7	52.9	48.1
Looking after home	20.1	11.6	30.3	34.9
Permanently sick or disabled	3.1	0.9	1.7	1.5
Other	9.3	6.5	15.0	15.4
Aged 25 and over				
Economically active	100.0	100.0	100.0	100.0
Employed part-time	38.8	25.5	30.5	29.3
Employed full-time	49.0	57.2	43.9	43.9
Self-employed part-time	4.1	3.1	4.0	2.8
Self-employed full-time	4.3	7.6	6.1	3.6
Unemployed	3.2	5.8	13.5	17.3
Student	0.6	0.8	2.1	3.0
Economically inactive	100.0	100.0	100.0	100.0
Retired	47.4	23.8	7.6	6.0
Student	1.5	2.5	2.0	1.8
Looking after home	29.7	40.5	58.6	61.1
Permanently sick or disabled	14.0	16.7	10.7	7.4
Other	7.3	16.5	21.1	23.6

Note: Percentages may not total 100 due to rounding.

Source: Census 2001 National Report for England and Wales, table S108

Table A3: Gender and occupation by ethnic group, England and Wales, 2001 (%)

	White British		Indian		Pakistani		Bangladeshi	
	Males	Females	Males	Females	Males	Females	Males	Females
Managers	18.5	11.1	20.7	11.5	14.0	8.6	14.3	5.9
Professionals	11.6	9.5	20.3	12.9	11.3	12.8	8.3	11.4
Associate professionals	13.6	13.7	10.1	11.9	7.4	10.9	5.7	10.5
Administrative	5.3	23.0	7.5	21.7	6.1	20.0	5.5	22.4
Skilled trades	20.3	2.4	9.9	1.7	9.2	1.3	24.3	2.2
Personal service	2.0	12.9	1.3	6.0	1.6	11.4	1.3	12.2
Sales	3.8	12.1	7.9	14.6	10.3	18.8	9.6	21.8
Process operatives	13.3	3.1	12.2	8.6	25.0	5.7	8.3	3.9
Elementary occupations	11.8	12.1	10.0	10.9	15.2	10.5	22.9	9.6

Source: Census 2001, National Report for England and Wales, table S109

Table A4: Social class position of women from selected ethnic groups with level 4/5 education, England, Wales and Northern Ireland, 2001 (%)

Ethnic group		
White British	I Professional, etc.	10.1
	Ii Managerial and technical	65.8
	Iii N Skilled – non-manual	15.3
	Iii M Skilled – manual	4.6
	Iv Partly skilled	3.9
	V Unskilled	0.4
	Total	100.0
	Total N	*78,971*
Indian	I Professional, etc.	19.6
	Ii Managerial and technical	44.5
	Iii N Skilled – non-manual	26.0
	Iii M Skilled – manual	4.5
	Iv Partly skilled	4.9
	V Unskilled	0.4
	Total	100.0
	Total N	*2,748*
Pakistani	I Professional, etc.	16.5
	Ii Managerial and technical	43.9
	Iii N Skilled – non-manual	26.8
	Iii M Skilled – manual	3.3
	Iv Partly skilled	9.0
	V Unskilled	0.5
	Total	100.0
	Total N	*665*
Bangladeshi	I Professional, etc.	16.0
	Ii Managerial and technical	44.2
	Iii N Skilled – non-manual	26.5
	Iii M Skilled – manual	5.5
	Iv Partly skilled	7.2
	V Unskilled	0.6
	Total	100.0
	Total N	*181*

Note: Percentages may not total 100 due to rounding.
Source: Sample of Anonymised Records

Table A5: All women aged 18–24 by selected ethnic groups, England and Wales, 1991–2001

	1991	2001	% change 1991–2001
White	2,367,544	1,898,094	-19.8
Indian	50,204	64,905	29.3
Pakistani	31,278	54,318	73.7
Bangladeshi	10,322	23,382	126.5

Source: Census of Population 1991 and 2001

Table A6: Percentages within sexes, home applicants and degree acceptances by gender and selected ethnic groups, England and Wales, 2003 entry

| | | Ethnic origin | | | |
		Bangladeshi	Indian	Pakistani	White
Percentage of 16-24 age group in 2001	Females	1.1	2.9	2.5	82.4
	Males	0.9	2.9	2.4	83.6
Percentage of applicants in 2003	Females	0.8	4.2	2.4	72.5
	Males	1.0	4.9	3.3	69.0
Percentage of degree acceptances	Females	0.8	4.4	2.3	73.9
	Males	0.9	5.1	3.0	70.7
Representation of applicants in 2003	Females	0.77	1.44	0.98	0.88
	Males	1.14	1.72	1.40	0.83
Representation of degree acceptances	Females	0.73	1.51	0.93	0.90
	Males	1.06	1.77	1.25	0.85

Notes: Tables A6 and A7 show how far young South Asian women were over- or under-represented in applications and acceptances to university in 2003 for England and Wales. The second section of each table contains representation quotients calculated from the percentages. If a group was represented equally among both the applicants and the age group then its representation quotient would be 1.00, if it was under-represented it would be less than 1.00 and over-represented it would be greater than 1.00. The first of these tables focuses on ethnic differences within each gender, that is, ethnic differences between female applicants for example. The second presents the data looking at gender differences within each ethnic group.
Source: 16-24 age group data Census of Population, 2001; applicants and degree acceptances, UCAS

Table A7: Percentages within ethnic groups, home applicants and degree acceptances by gender and selected ethnic groups, England and Wales, 2003 entry

| | | Ethnic origin | | | |
		Bangladeshi	Indian	Pakistani	White
Percentage of 16-24 age group in 2001	Females	53.9	50.3	50.4	49.3
	Males	46.1	49.7	49.6	50.7
Percentage of applicants in 2003	Females	48.5	50.2	46.0	55.3
	Males	51.5	49.8	54.0	44.7
Percentage of degree acceptances	Females	49.4	50.9	47.6	55.5
	Males	50.6	49.1	52.4	44.5
Representation of applicants in 2003	Females	0.90	1.00	0.91	1.12
	Males	1.12	1.00	1.09	0.88
Representation of degree acceptances	Females	0.92	1.01	0.94	1.12
	Males	1.10	0.99	1.06	0.88

Source: 16-24 age group data: Census of Population, 2001; applicants and degree acceptances: UCAS

Table A8: Female degree applicants for selected ethnic groups by JACS subject group, 2005 entry (%)

JACS subject group	Ethnic origin			
	Bangladeshi	Indian	Pakistani	White
Group A Medicine & Dentistry	7.0	11.4	10.2	3.2
Group B Subjects allied to Medicine	10.9	14.4	14.7	11.9
Group C Biological Sciences	7.0	6.7	5.3	8.5
Group D Veterinary Science, Agriculture & related	0.1	0.1	0.0	1.4
Group F Physical Sciences	0.9	1.0	0.7	2.4
Group G Mathematical & Computer Sciences	4.2	3.9	4.7	1.4
Group H Engineering	0.4	0.6	0.5	0.6
Group J Technologies	0.0	0.1	0.0	0.1
Group K Architecture, Building & Planning	0.6	0.8	0.3	0.7
Group L Social Studies	9.9	6.6	7.5	7.5
Group M Law	11.6	9.1	12.2	4.1
Group N Business & Administrative studies	13.0	16.6	14.2	6.9
Group P Mass Comms and Documentation	2.0	1.9	1.0	2.2
Group Q Linguistics, Classics & related	3.2	1.8	1.3	3.9
Group R European Langs, Literature & related	0.2	0.4	0.2	1.4
Group T Non-European Languages and related	0.3	0.1	0.4	0.3
Group V History & Philosophical studies	1.8	0.9	0.9	3.5
Group W Creative Arts & Design	5.0	6.2	3.5	14.4
Group X Education	6.8	2.6	5.3	6.7
Y Combined arts	0.6	0.9	1.0	2.9
Y Combined sciences	0.1	0.1	0.1	0.4
Y Combined social sciences	0.9	0.8	0.8	0.5
Y Sciences combined with social sciences or arts	1.4	1.9	1.5	2.1
Y Social sciences combined with arts	0.6	1.2	0.6	1.7
Z General, other combined & unknown	0.4	0.1	0.2	0.3
Z No preferred subject group	11.1	9.7	12.7	11.1
Grand total	100.0	100.0	100.0	100.0
Total N	1,874	8,645	5,723	191,560

Note: Percentages may not total 100 due to rounding.

Source: UCAS, authors' analysis

Table A9: Female degree acceptances for selected ethnic groups by JACS subject group, 2005 entry (%)

JACS subject group	Ethnic origin			
	Bangladeshi	Indian	Pakistani	White
Group A Medicine & Dentistry	2.9	6.7	4.3	2.2
Group B Subjects allied to Medicine	9.2	13.9	15.0	9.5
Group C Biological Sciences	8.5	8.1	7.3	10.0
Group D Veterinary Science, Agriculture & related	0.1	0.3	0.1	1.5
Group F Physical Sciences	1.4	1.6	1.7	3.2
Group G Mathematical & Computer Sciences	6.4	4.8	6.2	1.8
Group H Engineering	0.9	1.2	1.0	0.8
Group J Technologies	0.1	0.3	0.2	0.3
Group K Architecture, Building & Planning	0.8	0.9	0.5	1.0
Group L Social Studies	11.4	7.5	8.5	8.0
Group M Law	12.8	9.6	13.4	4.8
Group N Business & Administrative studies	12.5	16.8	14.0	7.7
Group P Mass Comms and Documentation	2.0	2.2	1.3	2.6
Group Q Linguistics, Classics & related	3.9	1.9	2.0	4.6
Group R European Langs, Literature & related	0.1	0.5	0.1	1.7
Group T Non-European Languages and related	0.1	0.2	0.5	0.6
Group V History & Philosophical studies	2.3	1.2	1.2	4.1
Group W Creative Arts & Design	4.2	5.4	3.2	13.1
Group X Education	5.5	2.6	5.0	6.3
Y Combined arts	2.6	1.7	2.0	4.7
Y Combined sciences	1.2	1.5	1.1	1.4
Y Combined social sciences	3.0	2.3	2.4	1.1
Y Sciences combined with social sciences or arts	3.7	4.9	4.6	4.6
Y Social sciences combined with arts	2.2	2.4	1.9	3.0
Z General, other combined & unknown	2.2	1.7	2.4	1.4
Z No preferred subject group	0.0	0.0	0.0	0.0
Grand total	100.0	100.0	100.0	100.0
Total N	1,419	7,019	4,135	150,537

Note: Percentages may not total 100 due to rounding.

Source: UCAS, authors' analysis

Table A10: Two or more A-levels by gender for selected ethnic groups, 2002 (%)

	White	Indian	Pakistani	Bangladeshi
Males				
2+ A-levels	44.6	61.4	23.6	25.0
Less than 2+ A-levels	55.4	38.6	76.4	75.0
N	*2,641*	*88*	*55*	*28*
Females				
2+ A-levels	49.7	64.9	34.3	34.4
Less than 2+ A-levels	50.3	35.1	65.7	65.6
N	*3,691*	*131*	*99*	*32*

Source: Youth Cohort Study, 2002, authors' analysis.

Table A11: UK domiciled students by gender and ethnic group for universities in or near the study areas 2003–04 (%)

Ethnicity	Gender	Leeds	LMU	Birmingham	Aston	UCE	Wolverhampton
White	Female	50.6	44.3	36.8	26.3	41.8	43.5
	Male	36.3	34.5	25.6	27.2	23.5	24.9
Black	Female	0.9	1.3	1.6	1.8	7.1	4.2
	Male	0.6	1.2	0.9	1.5	3.4	2.2
Asian	Female	3.1	3.6	5.9	19.3	9.5	8.9
	Male	2.6	4.7	5.0	19.8	9.9	8.3
Other	Female	1.5	0.8	1.2	1.3	1.9	1.2
	Male	0.9	0.7	0.8	1.3	0.9	0.7
Unknown	Female	1.9	5.0	12.9	0.5	1.1	3.1
	Male	1.6	3.8	9.2	1.0	1.0	3.0
Total		100.0	100.0	100.0	100.0	100.0	100.0

Note: Percentages may not total 100 due to rounding.
Source: HESA (2006)